Gourmet Customer Service

A Scientific Approach to Improving the Caller Experience

by Peter Leppik and David Leppik

Illustrated by Jennifer Steadman

VocaLabs

VOCAL LABORATORIES INC.

Discounts on this book are available for bulk orders and special sales. For more information, please contact:

Vocal Laboratories Inc.
10925 Valley View Rd., Suite 202
Eden Prairie, MN 55344
sales@vocalabs.com

VOCAL LABORATORIES INC.

ISBN 0-9764055-0-4

First printing, January 2005

Special Thanks to
Jim Larson, Rick Rappé
and
Carla Hennes, Sue Fairchild, Richard Sachs,
Walt Tetschner, and Richard Rosinski

Contents

Foreword
by Jim Larson
Manager, Advanced Human I/O, Intel Corporation
Program Chair, SpeechTEK Conference
Co-chair, W3C Voice Browser Working Group

This book will have a significant impact on the call center industry by explaining how testing—often an afterthought—can be integrated with the design and operation of call centers and customer service automation, yielding a much improved call experience *and* reduced costs.

One of the greatest tragedies is to spend months or years developing a call center application that is seldom used because callers don't understand it. One of the largest mistakes managers make is to postpone usability testing until the end of a project, when there is little time or resources left to modify the user interface.

New tools for developing customer service automation are appearing almost daily. Reusable components promise to decrease the time and effort to create applications. Unfortunately, these tools and components also enable engineers to develop poor applications faster and more efficiently.

What's the solution to these problems?

i

Testing.

This is a book about a scientific approach to improving customer service. The only certain way to make the caller's experience better is to gather meaningful data, experiment with changes, and collect more data to find out what the effect was.

Testing is not an afterthought. It is an integral part of designing and operating any call center technology where improved service is a goal.

It is possible to discover and resolve problems before your customers discover them for you. But you must select the proper tests and apply them at the proper time. You can bootstrap your call center out of the sea of mediocre customer service into a world-class operation that enables your callers to perform their tasks quickly and easily. When you accomplish this, your callers will become your loyal customers.

James A. Larson
December, 2004

Introduction
by Rick Rappé
Vice President- Business Development
Vocal Laboratories Inc.

This book advocates a new approach to assessing customer service performance, one that uses data gathering, experimentation, and a scientific mentality to provide your customers with the best and most cost-effective service possible. If you're a professional in the call center world, we hope this book will open your eyes to how much better things can be than the poor service we have all experienced. In the research we've done at Vocal Laboratories, we've found some remarkable things:

- Good service isn't more expensive than bad service.

- Customers often prefer automated self-service, if it meets their needs.

- Call centers can be more important to brand image than advertising.

If you're looking for quick fixes and immediate answers to every one of your customer service problems, you won't find them here. This book is about a systematic process for improving your customer service, centered on rigorous data collection and a scientific mindset.

The authors, Peter and David Leppik, cofounded VocaLabs after realizing that advances in call center technology were not often translating into improvements in customer service.

One reason is that technology is often deployed with a focus on lowering costs, not improving the caller's experience. But perhaps even more significant, few companies analyze the quality of their customer service using rigorous methods and a formal program of continuous quality improvement. In fact, some popular techniques for measuring caller satisfaction amount to little more than "satisfaction snake-oil." As call center technology advances, a more sophisticated approach is needed.

There are many reasons testing is often inadequate, and this book is intended to help companies understand both the "why" and the "how" of measuring the quality of customer service. This book is not intended to get into the nitty-gritty of every measurement technique, but rather give you enough information to understand the basic issues, common pitfalls, and things to watch out for. We hope to make you an informed consumer of the data you use to measure your call center. If you need more depth, there are resources (see *For Further Reading* in the back of this book) where you can learn more about many of the topics we cover.

This book is primarily focused on phone-based customer care. This doesn't mean other customer service channels, such as E-mail, web pages, and on-line chats, are unimportant. The ideas of this book are just as applicable to these channels, and some of the techniques can be used with only minor tweaking in non-phone-based customer contacts.

The title and theme of this book is "Gourmet Customer Service," which describes what we hope you will achieve. Techniques used in measuring and improving customer service quality are the ingredients, which get combined into recipes for different situations you may face. And just as a chef will

iv

combine different dishes to make anything from a casual picnic lunch to an eight-course meal, we end the book with a discussion of how to deploy testing throughout the technology lifecycle in your call center to ensure that all your customers get the level of service they deserve.

Rick Rappé
December, 2004

Part 1:
What Is Gourmet
Customer Service?

The past twenty years have seen enormous change in call centers. A revolution in technology has allowed companies to dramatically increase their productivity from the days when every call had to be answered immediately by a person.

Similar improvements in business processes, such as deploying powerful database software, have led to even more productivity gains.

On the whole, these changes have been good for companies.

Customers, on the other hand, haven't always seen the benefits. Many long for the days when every call would be answered by a person before the third ring.

Without a new revolution in technology, the only way to continue to improve productivity is to bring callers into the process, making their goals the same as the call center's.

Callers don't care about your productivity targets, they only care about resolving their problems. You can force customers to use automated systems, but that only works for so long: people are smarter than machines, and they will figure out how to get what they want or go elsewhere out of frustration.

Improving both customer satisfaction and call center efficiency requires seducing the caller into using the most cost-effective service option. That means making self-service the most attractive route when self-service is appropriate; and encouraging callers to quickly go to live help when that's the best way to solve their problems.

Gourmet Customer Service is about providing the caller with an experience that is both attractive and efficient. Just as a gourmet meal does more than merely meet your nutritional needs, gourmet customer service goes beyond merely solving the caller's immediate problem. Gourmet Customer Service lets the call center both improve satisfaction and save money by aligning the customer's goals with the company's goals.

Saying you can both improve service and save money is easy. Doing it requires hard work and a methodical technique. The scientific approach we advocate uses hard data and a rigorous test regimen to discover what callers want and need, and validate the best way to meet those wants and needs.

Many companies already spend considerable time and effort measuring the performance of their call centers. Unfortunately, few of these companies take a scientific approach to understanding what they want to measure, gathering sufficient and meaningful data, and then acting upon the data in the appropriate fashion.

In Part 1 of this book, we outline some of the shortcomings we often see in quality improvement programs, and provide a systematic approach to improving service that avoids these problems.

Educating the Customer Service Palate

Let's just take it as given that no company wants to provide bad service.

There are companies that place more of a priority on cutting expenses than improving service, and there are employees who simply don't care about their jobs. But no sane executive charges his employees with making service worse. No company proudly announces "The Worst Customer Service in the Business" in its advertising.

So why is it that many customers often feel like companies don't want to do business with them?

In many cases, companies believe they're providing good service, but they're relying on poor-quality or misleading data. They've been providing customers with "junk food" service, thinking that meeting the customers' minimal needs is enough.

There are a lot of myths and bad ideas about measuring and improving customer service. Nearly every program for improving customer service we've seen suffers from at least one of these five flaws:

1: Failing to Ask Customers

Everyone has an opinion about customer service, and some of those opinions come with impressive credentials: PhD's, years of call center experience, and mountains of statistical data. Experts usually provide good ideas, but occasionally provide bad ones. Without direct caller feedback, there's no reliable way to tell the difference.

Large companies think nothing of spending thousands or millions of dollars on testing a new product. Customer service is an integral part of any company's product or service, and needs to be evaluated with the same level of rigor.

2: Failing to Gather Meaningful Data

The typical call center is a miniature data factory. Average time on hold, average call length, abandon rate, IVR containment rate, follow-up surveys, and call recordings are just some of the data generated every day.

This information is important, but it is critical to place it in the context of the company's business goals. There may be one agent who handles twice as many calls as average, but that doesn't mean she's providing good service. Maybe she's just transferring or hanging up when she gets a difficult question.

Meaningful data relates directly to the business goals of the call center, such as retaining customers or achieving a high level of single call problem resolution. A meaningful piece of data might be that 80% of your callers get the information they want on the first call,✱ or that your customers are 15% more likely to recommend your company to a friend after the call than before.

> An 80% successful single-call completion rate is about typical. In our research, we measure this by both asking callers if they got the information they wanted, and tracking which callers had to call more than once. The best score we've ever seen is 94%.

3: Failing to Gather Enough Data

Data is only significant when there is enough of it to reach a specific conclusion. For example, you may have a caller satisfaction rate of 70% in April, and 80% in May. If that's based on surveys of only 100 customers each month, then you can't conclude that your satisfaction level is improving. The change could easily be due to a difference in who you asked.

Figuring out when data is statistically significant doesn't have to be hard (see Appendix A: *Nobody Reads an Appendix on Statistics*), but it is vitally important. Imagine trying to land a 747 in a rainstorm using only a cheap compass that tells you you're going "Northish" or "More West than East"—or just swings wildly from side to side! That's the equivalent of trying to make important business decisions without enough data.

4: Failing to Understand the Data

By itself, most performance data for a call center is open to different interpretations. Without the complete picture, it is impossible to make informed business decisions.

For example, if you survey people who call your call center and 60% report that they are "Satisfied" or "Very Satisfied" with the experience, you might be inclined to pat yourself on the back and hand out bonuses. That is, unless you happen to know that in the *average* call center, nearly 70% of callers report being "Satisfied" or "Very Satisfied."✱ In order to be in the top quartile of call center operations, you have to have 85% or more of your callers report being "Satisfied" or better.

✱ The "Satisfaction" question has a strong upward bias. People tend to say that they're "satisfied" even when the experience was underwhelming. See Appendix A: *Nobody Reads an Appendix on Statistics* for more background on question bias.

Fully understanding the data you're generating requires that you know how it fits into the context of past performance, business goals, and industry benchmarks. Fully understanding the data means knowing not just the raw numbers, but why you are getting those results, and the ways the data could be misleading.

5: Failing to Use the Data

Knowing how to improve your customer service is good, but without a commitment to improve, good ideas get lost in the operational minutiae of running a call center. Sometimes simple changes—such as re-recording a menu in an IVR system—can have a big impact on performance and caller satisfaction. Even easy improvements might not get made if management has other priorities.

A commitment to continuous improvement is important. Without it, the only time significant changes get made is when there is a crisis, and a crisis is not the right time to make careful, sober decisions.

Constantly looking for small, simple improvements, and measuring the results not only maximizes the return on investments, but also creates the proper mindset for delivering outstanding service.

A Scientific Approach to Gourmet Customer Service

Call center automation is by its nature a form of artificial intelligence. It puts a talking machine in the role of a person. Even the humble answering machine augments the role of a secretary, and today's systems can automate even complex transactions.

The natural starting point for a scientific approach to improving customer service is research that has been done on human/computer interaction, generically called "usability."

Most usability research relates to how people use graphical user interfaces (GUIs) in desktop software and web sites, but people use GUIs very differently than they use telephones. Whether you are typing, clicking on buttons, or dragging an icon, in a GUI the metaphor is that of a physical environment: a place where you can touch and move things. You can type into a word processor, but you can't reason with it.

Voice User Interfaces (VUIs) are different. When the talking stops, there's only silence. If you didn't hear your options the first time, you must ask to have them repeated. The metaphor is a conversation. Like a conversation between two people, a caller interacting with a VUI will take cues from both what the system says and how the system says it.

Despite the differences between GUIs and VUIs, we can learn a lot from GUI-focused usability research. Measuring the quality of the call experience evaluates both live agents and software, and it doesn't matter much whether we label it "customer service" or "usability." The core ideas from usability research are just as applicable to customer service operations:

- Experience and expertise is good, but can't replace data from actual callers.

- Test a design as early as possible, and iterate through many designs.

- Tests should be as realistic as possible, and reflect what actual callers will know and do in the real world.

- Feedback from tests needs to be incorporated into the design as quickly as possible.

- Company employees, designers, and programmers don't do a good job finding problems. This is not because they aren't smart enough, but because they know too much about how the service is supposed to work.

The Scientific Approach

Step 1: Set Goals Decide what you hope to achieve. Use relevant business goals, such as increasing caller satisfaction or lowering the cost of service, rather than proxies like reducing average time on hold. Goals can be relative ("increase satisfaction") or absolute ("90% first-call resolution"), but they should be measurable.

Step 2: Gather Data Design a test regimen that will both measure where you are relative to your goals, and provide insight into ways to achieve those goals. Multiple kinds of tests may be required to give a complete picture.

Step 3: Take Action Design and implement changes to your customer service operation that you believe will move you closer to your goals. Be flexible, and do some experimentation to find the best approach.

Step 4: Validate Repeat some or all of the tests from Step 2 to make sure the changes had the desired effect. This step is essential, since some changes won't work the way you expected. You may have to return to Step 3 occasionally.

Step 5: Commit Providing Gourmet Customer Service is an ongoing process, not a one-time change. Go back to Step 1, update your goals based on what you learned, and look for more ways to improve.

- Small changes can have a big impact—for better or for worse.

Together, these core concepts form the foundation of a scientific approach to improving customer service. We call it "scientific" because the heart of the approach is using data gathered from real callers to improve customer service, as opposed to expert opinions, rules of thumb, the management-fad-of-the-week, or relying on vendors' marketing claims.

When adopting this approach, call centers have some important advantages over the GUI-based usability research we're borrowing from. A large-scale test (1,000 or more test participants) of a call center is much simpler and less expensive than a similar study of a new spreadsheet or e-mail program. This is because having test participants call from a convenient location is both cheaper and more realistic than bringing participants into a lab.

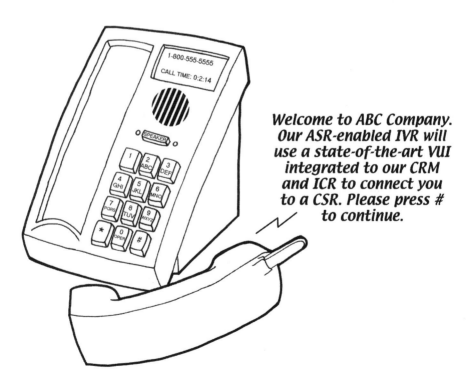

Welcome to ABC Company. Our ASR-enabled IVR will use a state-of-the-art VUI integrated to our CRM and ICR to connect you to a CSR. Please press # to continue.

Testing Customer Service

Testing is based on two radical notions. First, that you aren't the same as your callers, whether you are a software developer or a call center manager. And second, even if you know your callers better than they know themselves, you don't know how they will react when they call. The mark of a seasoned call center testing expert is humility.

Details are crucial. Sometimes a single word is the difference between success and mass confusion. And a system that works great when called from a quiet office might prove worthless when called from a noisy shopping mall. You just can't assume that it will work unless you test it.

Testing can help you understand a caller's *mental model*—the way the caller perceives the call center, as opposed to how an insider sees it. An employee or consultant will have more information about how the call center works and how to achieve a desired goal than any actual customer. This can make it difficult for an insider to get inside the head of the caller.

Usability Tests

A usability test is a study of how easy it is for people to use a computer program, and there are a number of different ways to do one. The purpose is to bring opinions of users into the design process.

Because of the prevalence of graphical user interfaces (or GUIs for short), most usability testing techniques have been designed with GUIs in mind. Since GUIs are by definition *graphical*, the visual element is normally the most important thing being tested. A typical test will bring participants into a lab where they are given a prototype of the GUI, and asked to perform common tasks such as opening a file, formatting a document, or finding information. The researchers collect data about the GUI by both observing the participants and asking for feedback.

Unfortunately, this exact methodology doesn't work well for call centers, both because it is very expensive to bring people into a lab (hence the studies tend to be very small), and because a lab is not a realistic environment for making phone calls. Fortunately, there are approaches that do work for the customer service environment, which we discuss in Chapter 7, *Controlled Testing (Including Usability Tests)*.

Mental model problems can crop up in many ways. If you use a shopping cart metaphor for a self-service system, the caller had better understand the metaphor. Before you ask a caller if he wants to "recharge" his prepaid wireless phone, you should be certain that he won't think you're talking about plugging it

Jargon

A common problem we see when testing an automated system—whether a state of the art VUI or a glorified answering machine—is jargon. It's also a problem for live agents, but less so since they quickly learn to talk around it.

Jargon is any industry or company-specific terminology that your callers don't understand. It can be subtle, since some words have specific technical meanings, but slightly different meanings in everyday speech.

Consider the word "serving," which has a precise definition to nutritionists. You could talk with a nutritionist for hours before realizing that you meant "a plateful" of pasta and she meant "half a cup."

into the wall. At the very least, you shouldn't inadvertently reinforce a misleading mental model.

In addition to finding conceptual misunderstandings, testing can also find specific flaws, such as badly timed prompts or poorly tuned speech recognition. What constitutes a flaw depends both on the caller and the application: speech recognition that works great in Minneapolis might be befuddled by the accents in New Orleans. If it turns out that people are calling from noisy day care centers or construction sites, the flaw might be deciding to use speech recognition in the first place.

But Wait, There's More

The scientific approach isn't limited to finding problems with your customer service. Rigorous measurement and statistically meaningful data will allow you to broaden the horizons of your abilities to make informed business decisions. For example, you can learn:

- Whether your customer service is better than your competition's and why.

- If a new speech recognition system will live up to the vendor's claims—before you spend the money to deploy it.

- How much a change in your agent's training improved customer service, or whether service actually got worse.

- What low-cost (or no-cost) changes you can make to improve service levels.

- How much impact your call center has on your brand image and customer retention.

Part 2: Know Your Ingredients

Applying the scientific approach to improving customer service requires combining techniques and test methods to get the best data in the most efficient and cost-effective way possible. There are almost as many ways to measure the performance of a call center as there are consultants selling performance assessment services. Some techniques are more flexible than others, some are more accurate than others, and some are cheaper than others. No one method works in every situation, so it is important to be familiar with several different test methods, just as a gourmet chef keeps many ingredients in a well-stocked pantry.

In this section, we'll introduce you to the most common assessment techniques, and some other important ingredients like statistics and prototyping. Since not every ingredient is appropriate for every situation, we've labeled each technique to help guide you in deciding where it should be applied.

 These ingredients are **fundamental** to the scientific approach. An understanding of these concepts is important to success.

These ingredients are most applicable to **automated customer service** operations, rather than agent-based call centers.

 These ingredients are best used for **live-agent** call centers, rather than automated customer service.

 These ingredients work best in a **larger customer service operation**. Smaller call centers may find that these techniques are difficult to implement or are not cost-effective.

 These ingredients are **Not Recommended**, even though they may be common in the real world. Not Recommended usually means that a technique gives misleading results, or is rarely implemented properly in practice.

Didn't anybody test it before today?!?

Automated Customer Service: The Project Lifecycle

There are some additional considerations when deploying a new piece of technology in a customer service operation. Any technology implementation goes through six phases in the lifecycle from conception through deployment to obsolescence, and some techniques are suitable only for certain project phases.

 These ingredients are most suited for the **analysis phase** of a project, where you're determining the requirements and scope.

 These ingredients are best used in the **design stage** of a project, where the details of a voice user interface are being determined.

 These ingredients are most appropriate for use in the **test phase**, where the software is being debugged and prepared for deployment.

These ingredients should be used primarily in a system that is **operational** and accepting live customer calls.

The section *Gourmet Meal Planning: The Life of an Automated System* discusses the project lifecycle in more detail, along with suggestions for developing a test regimen throughout the life of a piece of technology.

17

Statistics

FUNDAMENTAL

What is it?

Properly understanding how to measure and improve the quality of customer service requires at least a basic understanding of the power and limitations of the most important tool: statistics. Knowledge of statistics is as important to creating gourmet customer service as a basic knowledge of slicing, mixing, and baking is to a gourmet chef. A complete overview of statistics is well beyond what we can provide in this book, but fortunately some basic statistical knowledge and a few rules of thumb are enough to avoid the most common traps.

In looking at statistics for measuring call center performance, we are interested in three things: Can we trust the data? Will the data tell us what we need to know? And do we have enough data?

Appendix A: *Nobody Reads an Appendix on Statistics* contains a discussion of the most common statistical pitfalls, as well as some rules of thumb about how big a study you need, and how to gather your data in a way that will make it as meaningful as possible. For those not familiar with the statistical concepts of margin of error, question bias, and selection bias, this appendix should be required reading.

When is it used?

• All the time.

Pitfalls

• The most common statistical pitfall is trying to draw conclusions from too little data. How much data is "enough" will depend on exactly what you're trying to accomplish; but data for benchmarking and comparisons usually needs to survey at least 500 people, while early refinement of a prototype may need as few as 30-50 participants. When your budget permits, more data is always better than less data.

Based on my sophisticated statistical analysis of calling patterns and customer surveys, the inescapable conclusion is that you need to spend more money on consultants.

- Inconsistent data is another common pitfall. Data for benchmarking or making comparisons needs to be as consistent as possible, to ensure that you are making apples-to-apples comparisons. Using self-reported data from other call centers as a benchmark is especially troublesome, since it can be extremely difficult to make sure everyone is reporting exactly the same data.

- Bias, both in the way survey questions are written and in the way calls are included or excluded in a study, can lead to misleading or worthless data. While it may be impossible to eliminate all bias, it is possible to understand the sources of bias and work around the limitations of your data collection technique.

Inconsistency

As an example of inconsistent data, take what seems to be a straightforward call center statistic: average time on hold per caller.

This statistic is commonly reported by Automatic Call Distributors (ACDs), but there are several different ways to calculate it. For example, does the calculation include completely automated calls that never go to a live agent? Including those calls will tend to lower average time on hold. Are callers who hang up while on hold (abandoned calls) included in the calculation? Including abandoned calls will also tend to lower average time on hold. What about calls that are transferred and have to wait on hold twice? Is that one call or two for purposes of calculating call stats?

Some of these decisions can have a large impact on calculated average time on hold, and if you calculate it one way while another call center does it a different way, then your statistics are not comparable.

Recommendations

Some people spend their entire careers working with statistics, but the three most important statistical considerations are Size, Consistency, and Bias.

When deciding the size of a study, the rule is always that more data is better, within the limits of your budget. You should always make sure the amount of data you collect is sufficient to measure what you intend to measure (see the next chapter, *Setting Test Goals*), and if it isn't, then the test method, budget, or goals may have to be adjusted. If you are relying on an outside vendor or consultant to design the test regimen, you should understand the reasons why the vendor or consultant is recommending the particular size study.

Consistency is key when you're trying to make any kind of comparisons, including comparing your performance to industry benchmarks, or even just your September performance to your August performance. This is particularly true when measuring opinions (such as caller satisfaction), but is even the case for seemingly straightforward technical metrics like average time on hold. If you are using a third party to supply benchmark or comparison data, you should understand where the vendor gets its data and the steps it takes to ensure that the data is "clean." Be careful of vendors who use self-reported data from other call centers as benchmarks, since ensuring consistency in self-reported data is especially difficult.

Finally, bias can never be completely eliminated, but it can be understood and controlled. The most important thing is to avoid survey questions or testing techniques that are obviously biased. From there, it is important to understand the limitations of the data, and work within those limitations. If you are working with a consultant or vendor, he or she should be able to help you understand the sources of bias in your particular data sets, and ensure that you can find techniques to meet your goals within the limits of the data you can collect.

Setting Test Goals

FUNDAMENTAL

What is it?

One of the most important steps in measuring the performance of a customer service operation is understanding exactly what you want to measure and why. Back in high school chemistry, before beginning an experiment you always had to devise a hypothesis: either a theory you hoped to test, or an idea of what you intended to learn from the experiment. The same principle applies when measuring customer service performance.

Surprisingly, this step is sometimes overlooked when companies decide to measure the performance of their call centers. There may be little more than a vague executive directive that "we should be listening to what customers say," or "we need to know if we're doing a good job or not," without much thought about what those goals mean.

A scientific approach always begins by deciding what data is important, and how it will be used. For example, it is very different to benchmark your call center performance so you can give bonuses to top-performing agents or managers, as compared to just making sure you're not doing anything disastrously wrong. An early prototype of a new speech recognition system requires one kind of test to make sure the design isn't fundamentally flawed; while a nearly complete system needs a more rigorous test to ensure that it meets design goals; and a deployed system demands a completely different kind of test to make sure it continues to operate properly.

When is it used?

•   All the time.

•   Before deciding the details of a particular test regimen.

Pitfalls

•   The biggest pitfall is usually failing to properly set test goals at all. The CEO says, "Go measure caller satisfaction," and

23

the call center manager finds the lowest bidder who claims to measure "satisfaction" without much thought as to how the data will be used or whether the particular measurement is relevant to the company's goals.

- The other common pitfall is setting more aggressive test goals than the budget (either time or money) will allow. This often leads the company to use inappropriate techniques, yielding misleading data.

Recommendations

Setting test goals does not have to be a formal process, especially for small tests, but it does need to be done. If your goal is to gather informal feedback about ways to improve, that's perfectly acceptable, and understanding that goal will both lead you to an appropriate data collection technique (ask agents for suggestions, or use a focus group) and help you understand the limits of the data you gathered (not statistically meaningful, nor useful for benchmarking and comparisons).

On the other hand, if your goal is to track overall caller satisfaction levels over time with a degree of statistical precision, you will need to choose a different test regimen, probably involving large-scale consumer surveys or regular controlled tests (see Chapter 8, *Surveying Past Callers*; and Chapter 7, *Controlled Testing*).

In some cases, the test may be intended to measure a very specific operational goal such as "85% of callers who want to transfer funds from one account to another should be able to complete the transaction on the first call without talking to an agent." This demands a very specific kind of test, probably a controlled test, and enough participants to ensure a statistically meaningful result. You will need to make sure (probably with the help of an outside consultant or vendor) that your test regimen not only measures exactly what you think it measures, but also has enough precision to ensure you're confident in the end results.

5 Prototyping

DESIGN STAGE

AUTOMATION

What is it?

Prototyping is an important tool for exploring different design decisions and gathering data about how well an automated system will work. There are two common types of prototypes for Voice User Interfaces (VUIs): Wizard of Oz (or WOZ) prototypes and working prototypes. Prototypes are normally used in conjunction with a controlled test to evaluate and validate design decisions (see Chapter 7, *Controlled Testing*).

Wizard of Oz (WOZ)

A Wizard of Oz (WOZ) prototype requires no software development at all. A test administrator pretends to be the automated system by playing recorded messages to test participants and listening to their responses.

Wizard of Oz has the advantage of being inexpensive to develop, though it is not cost-free: someone has to set up and run the test (of-

So named because a human pretends to be the speech recognition engine. Just like in the *Wizard of Oz* movie, the caller isn't supposed to look behind the curtain and see a person pretending to be an impressive feat of engineering.

ten an expensive usability expert), and some WOZ experts like to use messages recorded by professional voice talent. Keep in mind that WOZ focuses on flaws in the design rather than flaws in the implementation, since the human "wizard" will be more accurate than a real system in the real world.

A WOZ prototype has two advantages over a working prototype. First, if you're building a speech recognition system, a WOZ avoids having to tune the voice recognizer, an advantage that will diminish as speech recognition technology improves. And second, there's no temptation to re-use prototype software that may not be suitable for a production environment.

Historically, WOZ prototyping has been a common way to test speech recognition systems—so much so that many experts in the field use the term "WOZ test" to refer to any usability test of a prototype speech recognition system. With better development tools, many vendors now have the capability to build a complete working prototype speech application from scratch in a matter of days, and we expect working prototypes to become the method of choice for testing speech recognition systems.

Working Prototypes

A working prototype, as the name implies, is a prototype of the application that functions just like the real thing. It may be an early version of the actual IVR software, or a speech recognition application built in a rapid prototype environment, but the important consideration is that there's as little sleight of hand involved as possible. In a speech recognition system, callers will encounter actual speech recognition errors, and have to recover from them.

A working prototype takes more effort to construct than a WOZ, but it acts more like a real system. The major advantages are test flexibility and realism. It can handle multiple simultaneous calls, making test scheduling easier; and provides a level of performance closer to what you expect to find in the real world.

When is it used?

- To design a new VUI in conjunction with exploratory usability tests.

Pitfalls

- Time and realism must be balanced. If a prototype takes too long to create, there won't be time to do more prototyping if needed. If it isn't realistic, test results will be uninformative or misleading.

Recommendations

Working prototypes and WOZ have their advantages and disadvantages. We favor the working prototype, because it is generally more realistic and lends itself to larger-scale testing. Certainly for touch-tone applications, developing a working prototype is easier and cheaper than WOZ.

For speech recognition applications, WOZ has traditionally been the prototyping method of choice, simply because rapid prototyping tools didn't exist for speech. This is changing, however, and many vendors now have the capability to build rapid prototypes of speech-recognition systems. As the technology continues to advance, we think there will soon be little reason to choose WOZ over a working prototype.

Rules of Thumb, aka Heuristics

What is it?

Rules of thumb are used everywhere and for all kinds of customer service. If you follow a "do and don't" list when you make decisions in a customer service operation, you can avoid quite a few basic problems. Things like "best practices" check-lists, advice from consultants, and experience from wizened old call center managers are all common sources of good advice.

For example, a common rule of thumb in call centers is that if any call has been on hold for more than one minute (or 30 seconds, or five minutes, depending on the industry and the type of call center), then the queue is too long and immediate action must be taken.

Heuristics are a good way to avoid common problems, especially for inexperienced VUI designers and call center managers. And they are an easy way for the more experienced professional to keep opinionated but less-informed people from making ill-conceived requests.

But rules of thumb are not sufficient by themselves: not every rule is appropriate in every case, and you have to measure the effect of any decision to consider it part of a scientific approach to improving customer service. One study of web sites✱ found that while good heuristics are valuable, bad ones are actually harmful; and even good rules of thumb are not flexible enough to account for the details of a particular system.

✱ Evolution Trumps Usability Guidelines
By Jared M. Spool. 2002.
http://www.uie.com/articles/evolution_trumps_usability/

In the hold time rule of thumb, a blind adherence to the "one minute" rule might lead a call center manager to yank experienced agents out of an "escalation" queue to handle calls in the general queue. The "one-minute" crisis may be fixed, but at the cost of fewer experienced agents available to handle difficult calls or priority customers.

29

When is it used?

- To simplify design decisions.

- To avoid boneheaded mistakes.

- To generate a working hypothesis of how customer service can be improved.

Pitfalls

- Just because an expert says something doesn't mean it works in your case—or that it works at all. You need to understand the logic behind the rule of thumb, and measure the effect of applying it.

- Even the best heuristics aren't appropriate for every situation.

- Applying rules of thumb doesn't involve gathering any actual data from callers, but can give the illusion of "doing something" about a problem.

Recommendations

Since this book is about a scientific approach to improving customer service, we won't be spending much time discussing heuristics. That said, we don't want to leave the impression that expertise and rules of thumb are worthless. On the contrary, often these are the best starting places for ideas about how to improve service.

It is important to make sure that expert advice is just a starting point, and not the ending point. Ideas need to be validated with data, which means testing rather than just blindly applying the rules of thumb and hoping for the best.

7 Controlled Testing (Including Usability Testing)

What is it?

Controlled testing is the most powerful and flexible technique for learning how callers think about and use a call center, and it is a staple of the scientific approach. A controlled test focuses on the experience of an actual caller, usually a recruited study participant, making a call to the customer service operation under realistic but controlled circumstances.

Because of its focus on the caller, a controlled test can never be automated and shouldn't be performed using calls from consultants, call center agents, or other "professional testers." Controlled testing comes in a number of different variations, including mystery shopping, large-scale tests, lab tests, and rapid assessments.

A Controlled Test Has:

- Callers recruited for the test.
- One or more *scenarios* that describe the caller's task and pretended motivation.

Controlled testing is short for "controlled environment testing." The people calling, the reasons for the call, and the circumstances of the call are all under the control of the experimenter.

Types of Controlled Tests

All controlled tests have a similar structure: participants are given one or more things to accomplish by calling a call center, automated system, or prototype automated system. Callers' instructions, or "scenarios," can range from very simple to detailed and complex. Calls are normally recorded, and in a laboratory setting the participant may also be videotaped. After the call is complete, participants are asked for their opinions through a survey or interview.

All variations of controlled testing have three characteristics in common. First, while the calls and callers are as realistic as possible, they are not the same as "natural" calls. This allows you to control who calls and why, but you need to understand beforehand who real callers are and why they are really calling. Results can be misleading if the callers or scenarios are unrealistic.

Second, controlled tests center on each individual's own call experience, and participants don't share ideas with each other. A controlled test answers fundamental questions about participants' experiences such as: *How well does the system work? What percentage of callers are satisfied?* or *How often do people need to call back to complete their tasks?*

The most accurate information in a controlled test comes from gathering statistics from many different people. For example, *What percentage of callers experience a particular problem? How well does an IVR work with various demographic groups?* or *What percentage of people think the agents are really smart?*

Finally, controlled testing involves people. It measures human behavior as well as technical functionality, and it doesn't work without people.

Controlled test methods vary in the number of participants, the length of time the study takes, who the participants are, how realistic the test environment is, and what is being tested.

AUTOMATION

Usability Tests

A usability test is any controlled test intended to find usability problems: design flaws, bugs, and other problems that might prevent a caller from completing a task. This is as opposed to tests for other purposes like benchmarking or competitive analysis, though some kinds of controlled tests can be used for multiple purposes including usability. Rapid assessments, large scale tests, and lab tests (described below) are all suitable for usability testing.

A usability test is essentially a simple psychology experiment. If the test is done in a lab, it may even look like a psychology experiment, with the test facilitator (with or without a white lab coat) watching how well the participant can perform a set of tasks.

Historically, usability tests have often been done in a laboratory setting, largely because many usability experts got their start working with Graphical User Interfaces (GUIs). GUI testing is normally done in a lab, since the visual element is so important to the system.

Voice User Interfaces (VUIs) are different in that the most realistic test environment is to have participants call the system from their home or office. This allows a much larger and more cost-effective test method, since the test process can be largely automated and there is no cost or scheduling problem with a physical lab. As a result, the industry is moving away from lab-based usability testing and towards having participants call from convenient locations.

Mystery Shopping

Mystery shopping is based on a technique often used by retail stores. Retailers often hire someone to visit their own stores or a competitor's and report on the experience. Mystery shopping a call center usually involves calling a live-agent call center and reporting on the experience.

Some mystery shopping services use agents in one call center to call another call center. This can be useful if the goal is simply to make sure your call center agents are properly following a script or doing certain tasks during the call. If you want to measure callers' opinions about the call, a better approach is to use consumers as mystery shoppers, since their experience will more accurately reflect how an actual customer would think and feel during the call.

Unlike in the bricks-and-mortar environment, a mystery shopping program for a call center can record every call, providing an unbiased record of what actually happened during the interaction along with the opinions of the mystery shopper. This allows you to find out not just what happened during the call, but why.

Large-Scale Tests

LARGE CALL CENTER

Large-scale tests provide large numbers of participants and low per-participant costs. A typical test has at least 500 callers, and can be as large as 5,000. Participants are given instructions, a phone number to call, and a questionnaire. The burden on each participant is very low, usually a single call and a single questionnaire done without leaving home, and the total time from start to finish is often under ten minutes. As a result, the per-participant cost is often comparable to conducting an opinion survey of past callers (see Chapter 8: *Surveying Past Callers*), but with much more flexibility and depth of data.

A large-scale test is necessary to gather enough data to make statistically meaningful comparisons and benchmark calculations, and to provide a thorough evaluation of a call center or automated system. If you want to make sure that your speech recognizer can handle accents from all 50 states, a large number of test participants will be required, and a 1,000-person large-scale test will be the most cost-effective technique. It is possible to use a very select group of people with a large-scale test, but the per-participant cost advantage of this approach is weakened if screening or recruiting becomes expensive, or if one-on-one interviews are required.

Rapid Assessments

The Rapid Assessment is a shorter and time-limited version of a large-scale controlled test. Rapid Assessments were invented to overcome some of the limitations of lab tests while providing a more nimble approach than the large-scale test. Typically, rapid assessments do not need to be scheduled in advance, and are run for an hour or two. A rapid assessment can get dozens of responses in that time—an order of magnitude larger than lab tests, which can take weeks to schedule and run.

A rapid assessment depends on having a large database of potential participants available at any given time. Only a small percentage will participate, but if the pool is large enough, you'll

get enough. Participants fill out questionnaires rather than talk to a test administrator. All the administrator does is set up the instructions and questionnaire, make sure the application is up and running, and send out invitations to potential participants.

The main drawback is that there is very little control over the response rate: you might budget for thirty participants and end up with a hundred! Or you might expect a hundred but get only thirty. If a particular test's response is too low, you'll need to re-run it or extend its deadline.

Lab Tests

AUTOMATION

Lab tests take place in a laboratory setting, with participants in a room with a telephone, usually being observed or videotaped by the test administrator.

DESIGN STAGE

Even though lab tests are unrealistic for testing call centers and VUIs, they have the advantage of providing a lot more information about the thoughts and emotions of the participants. Facial expressions and gestures can be very revealing, and this information is simply not available in a call recording or survey.

Lab tests are a natural to use with Wizard of Oz (WOZ) prototypes, since WOZ requires a human operator for the test, and many test administrators prefer to be able to see the participant face-to-face.

The biggest practical disadvantages of a lab test are that they are expensive and difficult to schedule, often leading to small and infrequent testing. Where a rapid assessment can be done on demand and in an hour, involve dozens of participants, and cost a few hundred dollars, a typical lab test is a major undertaking costing thousands of dollars, weeks to perform including recruiting and scheduling, and rarely includes more than 20 participants.

When is it used?

- To audit and benchmark existing call centers.

- To tune up existing automated systems and look for usability problems.

- To test prototypes.

- As an acceptance test to guarantee the quality of a new automated system.

- To gather data for competitive analysis.

Pitfalls

- Unrealistic callers or unrealistic scenarios can lead to misleading results.

- Survey questions need to be constructed carefully to avoid bias.

Now that I have captured a live customer, I am ready to begin my experiments in customer service!

- Study participants may not behave exactly like real callers, so you may need to do "reality checks" depending on the goals of your testing.

Recommendations

Controlled testing will play a part in almost any test regimen, since it is often the most complete, cost-effective, flexible, and consistent way to gather data about how callers view a customer service operation. More than any other technique, a controlled test lets you experiment with your call center, so you can try different ideas and approaches to see what works best.

That said, controlled tests are not perfect, and there are lots of variations. The biggest problem is that test callers will rarely be exactly like real callers, so you need to be careful when extrapolating test results to the real world.

When deciding which of the many kinds of controlled test to perform, we generally recommend using the largest and most realistic test your time and budget will allow. Size is important, and you need at least several hundred participants to get good statistics and have a reasonable probability of finding most problems. Realism requires that you invest in good study design, a high-quality prototype (if appropriate), and use participants with skills and experience similar to actual callers (rather than call center agents or your employees) for the test. We generally recommend against lab tests, simply because rapid assessments are far more flexible and cost-effective, though there are usability professionals who would disagree with us on this point.

Surveying Past Callers

OPERATIONAL PHASE **LARGE CALL CENTER**

What is it?

The most direct way to find out what callers think is to ask them. Many call centers call customers back in order to ask questions about the service they received. This is a valuable information since you are asking real callers about real experiences, but there are drawbacks. Surveying is only possible if you have enough information about callers to contact them, and if the caller is willing to participate in the survey. This leads to a significant sample bias, and getting 10% of callers to take the survey is considered a good response rate.

In addition, unless the call was particularly memorable, people forget important details quickly, and may confuse that call with other calls, including calls to other companies. Memory starts to fade within minutes of hanging up. Because of this time lag, surveys are limited to general questions about the overall quality of the call. Callers should not be asked to remember specific events or details unless they can be surveyed within a very short time from when they hung up.

On the other hand, follow-up surveys can be especially useful for complex transactions such as reversing an erroneous charge on a monthly bill. In these situations, the goal is to find out whether the transaction was successfully completed, and the survey might not be done for a month or more after the call to give the customer time to make sure the problem was truly resolved.

Follow-up surveys are most useful for providing a reality check on other measurement techniques, since they are the best way to collect data from actual customers calling for their own purposes (as opposed to a controlled test). The limitations of this technique make it less useful for frequent monitoring, in-depth analysis, or uncovering specific problems.

When is it used?

- To evaluate the overall quality and impact of a call center.

Hello... amy smith...
Our records show you called ABC Company yesterday.
Would you like to take a brief 30-minute survey?

Honey, who's calling?

- As a reality check on other data.

Pitfalls

- Respondents will have forgotten details about the call, or may confuse it with other calls they have made.

- Survey response is often very low, 10% or less, meaning that large numbers of callers have to be contacted to get a reasonable sample.

- Selection bias is a big problem, since the vast majority of callers can't or won't participate. Those customers who do participate in the survey are more likely to hold extreme opinions.

- As with all surveys, question bias can be a problem, especially if the survey is administered by a live agent over the phone. See Appendix A, *Nobody Reads an Appendix on Statistics* for more about question bias.

- Statistically meaningful surveys (500 or more participants) can be expensive and take weeks to complete.

Recommendations

Follow-up surveys are an important tool, since they are the best way to make sure other data is giving an accurate picture of how customers really feel about your call center.

But in terms of the time and expense required to run a survey, and the relatively limited data that can be gathered, follow-up surveys are not very cost-effective.

As a result, we recommend using follow-up surveys as a way of validating other data collection techniques. Controlled tests are much more cost effective, so follow-up surveys should be performed mainly to make sure your controlled tests are giving an accurate picture.

End-of-Call Surveys

OPERATIONAL PHASE   **NOT RECOMMENDED**

What is it?

As we discussed in the prior chapter, surveying actual callers is an important way to gather information about your call center. Unfortunately, follow-up surveys can be time-consuming and expensive. In an attempt to cut costs and automate the process, some call centers are now asking callers to complete a questionnaire before they hang up.

These surveys are typically administered by asking the caller at the beginning of a call if he or she would like to take a short survey when the call is done. If the caller agrees, then when the agent or IVR hangs up, the call is transferred to the survey. Callers may be asked to enter their answers using the phone keypad, through speech recognition, or spoken answers may be recorded for later transcription.

The problem is that callers with the worst experiences will never get to the survey. Any caller who hangs up before the call is "finished" won't be able to take the survey, and those callers are the ones who most likely got confused, frustrated, or upset during the call.

In the worst case scenario—for example, when an automated system breaks completely, or when callers start abandoning calls in large numbers—this kind of survey will provide extremely misleading data, and may even show an improvement when things are going downhill.

There are some cases when an end-of-call questionnaire can be used, such as for augmenting a program of agent monitoring and coaching, or for engaging customers in a marketing promotion. But it won't be a representative sample of callers, and it can give the misleading impression of being meaningful data.

When is it used?

- For augmenting agent coaching or for promotional purposes, but not to gather meaningful statistics.

- When there are no alternative techniques available.

Pitfalls

- To participate, callers must:

  - Complete the call successfully.

  - Not hang up immediately.

  - Be willing to stay on the line.

- Results will be strongly biased.

- The usual survey pitfalls of biased questions and sample size also apply.

Recommendations

Because of the severe selection bias problems in end-of-call surveys, we strongly advise against using this method as part of a scientific approach to improving customer service.

Friends & Family (& Employee) Testing

AUTOMATION

NOT RECOMMENDED

What is it?

The cheapest and easiest way to test a new self-service system is to have someone convenient call in: friends, family, or employees. This technique is very common, but some of the worst call center automation we've ever evaluated was tested using only friends, family, and company employees.

Friends & Family testing has a number of problems: first, participants are often too much like you. If they are at all familiar with company or industry jargon, they'll have the same blind spots you do. They'll also have the same loyalties, and will hardly notice quirks or corporate flag-waving that real customers will find grating.

Friends & Family tests tend to reinforce preconceived notions shared by the call center insiders. These tests can actually be worse than no testing at all, since they can give an unwarranted confidence boost. Complicating matters, some participants will have an emotional or financial stake in the outcome, leading them to sugar-coat their true opinions.

Despite all the negatives, even we sometimes test on family and friends. The fact that it's free and can be done on a whim makes it hard to resist—plus we get to show off the fruits of our hard work. But don't treat the test as anything other than what it really is: a demonstration.

When it's used

*   As a cheap substitute for more realistic tests.

Pitfalls

*   Insiders are too familiar with your company's jargon and idiosyncrasies to notice them.

*   Insiders are too forgiving, or may have a stake in the outcome of the test.

- Insiders may be familiar with earlier prototypes—and might be blind to important omissions or (worse) may confuse earlier prototypes with more recent ones.

- Provides misleading data and an unwarranted sense of confidence that makes Friends & Family testing **worse than not testing at all**.

Recommendations

We recommend not using Friends & Family as a serious way to gather data about a call center or automated system. Be honest with yourself and call it a "demo."

11 Agent Feedback

OPERATIONAL PHASE

AGENTS

What is it?

Agents spend all day talking to customers, so they know what customers are thinking. When your product or service fails, agents are the first to hear about it. When customers expect your company to do something it doesn't do, agents hear about it. Innovative companies get their best ideas from their customers, and customer service representatives are an ideal conduit.

Unfortunately, many companies don't provide a meaningful channel of communication from the customer to the company through the call center. Customers often get the impression that the person answering the phone is not in a position to do something about a complaint or suggestion. Complaining to a call center agent may seem like it has no more impact than chatting with the barber.

Despite the importance of customer service representatives as a channel to the customer, agent feedback has three limitations. First, it requires live agents, so you won't get feedback about calls handled by an automated system. Second, agents will filter customer feedback, and any information about the agents themselves will be biased. Finally, the process for collecting feedback from agents has to be carefully handled so that agents won't feel they'll be penalized for being the bearers of bad news.

When is it used?

- Any live-agent call center

- For generating suggestions and ideas for improvement.

Pitfalls

- Great for generating feedback about the company, but limited for generating feedback about the call center.

- Does not generate quantitative data.

- Hard to apply in an outsourcing situation.

- Agents may be reluctant to offer honest opinions if they are worried about a "shoot the messenger" attitude from management.

Recommendations

Agent feedback is an inexpensive, powerful way to generate ideas, and every call center with customer service representatives should do it.

As a way of accurately measuring the whole range of customer opinions, however, it is limited. Agents only see some of the calls, and may be reluctant to offer their true opinions because of negative consequences of passing along bad news.

These limitations should be kept in mind, but they shouldn't discourage you from soliciting ideas and feedback from your customer service representatives.

Call Recording and Monitoring

OPERATIONAL PHASE

What is it?

Many call centers record some or all of their calls for a variety of reasons, including agent coaching, legal compliance, and improving IVR or speech recognition systems. Call recordings are also an integral part of controlled tests (see Chapter 7, *Controlled Testing*).

For this book, we're not concerned with legal compliance issues. But for quality assurance and improvement, call recordings are an invaluable tool.

When using call recordings for agent training, it is important to make sure the agent is being trained to help the caller solve problems, rather than simply follow a script or checklists. Scripts can be valuable for ensuring consistency, but agents must be allowed to do what is needed to help the customer in a courteous and efficient fashion.

Call recordings can also be helpful in improving automated systems, although listening to or transcribing large numbers of recordings can be expensive and time consuming. In order to avoid listening to hundreds of call recordings to find one trouble spot, the recordings should be used in combination with log analysis (see Chapter 15, *Call Logs and Call Stats*) to identify fruitful recordings for further analysis.

The biggest drawback is that a call recording only gives half the picture. It tells you what happened during the call, but not what the caller was trying to do, how she felt, or why she did what she did. This lack of insight into the caller's mindset is particularly limiting when using call recordings to improve automated systems, since an IVR (unlike an agent) will not make any attempt to establish rapport with the caller.

When is it used?

- Training and coaching live agents.

- Improving IVR and speech recognition systems.

- Legal compliance.

Pitfalls

- It only gives you half the information you need to understand the call, since you don't know what the caller was thinking or why.

- Call recordings are inherently qualitative, but some call centers and consultants turn this into quantitative data by scoring recordings on factors like "agent friendliness." It is usually more cost-effective and accurate to use a controlled test instead.

- Many call recordings include only the agent or automated part of a call. To be most useful, recordings should include the entire call from start to finish.

Recommendations

Listening to call recordings is probably the most common technique for call center quality assurance, although it is most often used for agent training rather than for identifying and fixing systematic problems.

Existing call recordings can be integrated into a larger program of customer service audits and improvements. To do this, you will need to regularly evaluate recordings for common service problems, and track whether making changes to a call center actually reduces the number of problems callers experience.

Where possible, it is best to use recordings that cover the entire call, including any time a caller spent on hold or inside an automated system. This will help identify problems related to agents, automation, transfers from department to department, or the combined impact of all of these together.

Automated Load Testing

OPERATIONAL PHASE   **CODE TEST PHASE**   **AUTOMATION**

What is it?

Automated load tests, sometimes called "stress tests," are essential when getting ready to deploy a new automated system. A computer is used to simulate dozens or hundreds of simultaneous calls, playing tones or recordings of people at appropriate times to simulate the actions of live callers.

This is far and away the most cost-effective way to make sure that a new system will be able to handle the expected call volume. Normally, a test is designed to cover major branches of the call flow, and the system is monitored to make sure it behaves correctly even when under heavy load.

Automated testing can also be used on an ongoing basis to alert call center managers to problems with their systems that might not be visible from inside the call center. For example, a test call every fifteen minutes can be used to watch for outages, misbehaving systems, and other technical problems.

When is it used?

- When testing a new automated system immediately before deployment.

- On an ongoing basis to monitor for technical failures or performance degradation.

Pitfalls

- An automated load test can't substitute for tests involving live callers, since the computer has no way of knowing how a human will react to the system.

Recommendations

Automated load testing should be part of the test regimen for any new piece of call center technology. There is simply no excuse for not doing it. A number of companies specialize in load testing, and many larger vendors of call center systems have the ability to do load testing in-house.

Traversal Testing

CODE TEST PHASE   **AUTOMATION**

What is it?

Traversal testing is a systematic way to make sure an automated system works the way the designers had intended. Engineers or testers call the system using a script that hits every point in the call flow—including error states—at least once. This will find places where the wrong recording was used, or where two recordings don't sound right when played together. This test can be automated to make sure the implementation meets the design specification, but it should be done at least once by a person to find problems with the recorded messages.

A traversal test should include every box and line on the call flow diagram. To be completely rigorous, this includes testing global options like "main menu" everywhere. Depending on how the system is programmed, that might seem like overkill—but before you cut corners, ask yourself: how else will this be tested?

When is it used?

- Before a new automated system is rolled out, or after changes are made to an existing system (see Chapter 19, *Acceptance Testing*).

- To make sure that every part of an automated system works as designed.

Pitfalls

- Traversal testing is a pain, so it can be tempting to skip it.

- Traversal testing does not substitute for usability testing because the scripted calls bear little resemblance to a typical caller making a typical call.

I'm not sure if this is a call flow diagram, or a map of an ant farm.

Whatever it is, it's your job to test it.

Recommendations

A complete traversal test should be part of the test regimen for any new automated system. A limited traversal test should be done every time a recording is changed, to make sure the recording works as expected in every situation. All it costs is a little bit of somebody's time, so there's no excuse for not doing it—no matter how small the application or budget.

Call Logs and Call Stats

What is it?

Automated call logs and real-time call statistics generated by a call center's telephone systems are often used to look for trouble spots and operational trends. This form of data collection is so basic that every call center, live agent or automated, should do it.

Logs and stats can provide information such as the average call length, time on hold, abandon rate, and call volume; as well as hints about what callers are looking for and whether they are finding it.

Unfortunately, this data only provides one side of the story, and can sometimes be misleading. For this reason, call logs and stats are best used as a tripwire for detecting changes, rather than for determining what those changes mean. As a tripwire, they are unbeatable: they capture every call and provide minute-to-minute updates.

57

Good log analysis is a balance between too much data and too little. Raw call logs hide valuable nuggets within reams of useless data, and reports that are too superficial will mislead by their lack of information. A two-tiered approach is useful: keep complete call logs with raw data in case you need it, and generate easy-to-read summary reports to provide a sense of the state of the system and signal changes. Data mining techniques can be valuable for spotting trends and problems that aren't obvious in the raw data.

In addition, new call center systems should be built to include logs that provide data directly relevant to the call center's performance. For example, logging the amount of time it takes each caller as well as the tasks the caller performed during the call gives a much more detailed picture of how well an automated system is performing. Errors should always be logged, though it is important to keep in mind that the caller's perception of an error may be different than what the automated system thinks is an error.

When is it used?

• As a tripwire when usage patterns change.

• To develop trend data for forecasting.

• As a tactical tool for hourly and daily call center management.

Managing to the Numbers

The great advantage of call logs and stats is that they are free and easy to generate in most call centers.

This advantage makes it very tempting to "manage to the numbers," and turn call stats into management goals excluding other factors that may be harder to measure.

For example, a call center that cares about caller satisfaction may use average time on hold as a proxy for caller satisfaction. This makes some sense, since spending a lot of time on hold is one of many things that can make callers dissatisfied.

But setting average time on hold as a primary goal can create perverse results. If there's a bonus for hitting a target, agents may be tempted to transfer or hang up on callers when they see the hold queue getting long. This will reduce average time on hold, but it won't help caller satisfaction.

Pitfalls

- This is not a replacement for gathering data from callers themselves. Managing to the stats can lead to poor service.

- Call logs and stats provide no context for interpreting the results: things that look bad in a log might be good, and vice-versa.

- Context is critical to understanding the data, but often overlooked.

Recommendations

Every call center should be gathering data through call logs and call stats, and nearly all do. This is the easiest form of data to collect about what's happening in a call center, and it can provide valuable insights into performance minute-by-minute.

Unfortunately, some call centers' data collection both begins and ends with logs and stats.

This data is most valuable for alerting you when something changes in a customer service operation—but it isn't always helpful in determining *what* changed, much less *why* and *what to do*.

For example, suppose the average call length suddenly jumps by a few seconds. This tells you that something has changed, but without further investigation, you don't know what. It could be because callers are using a new automated feature, because your database is responding sluggishly, or even because someone mistakenly filled the coffee pot with decaf that morning.

Part 3: Testing Recipes

In this section you'll find a number of common situations where you need to gather data on a customer service operation. Different goals lead to differences in the data you collect and how you analyze it.

Our recipes and the variations we suggest are a starting point to build your own test plan that fits your budget, timeline, and goals. Begin with the recipe that seems closest to what you hope to achieve, and make changes based on your own unique circumstances.

An **Audit** takes a detailed look at the quality of the customer service you provide, incorporating data from multiple sources. Just as a financial audit takes a detailed look at profit and loss and searches for signs of problems in a company's accounting, a customer service audit tells you how you're performing and looks for weaknesses you might not have known about.

Benchmarking is the classic "how are we doing?" study, comparing your performance against other call centers or tracking your call center over time. Benchmarks can be detailed or superficial, but always require careful attention to make sure you're comparing apples to apples.

Competitive Analysis is more detailed and specific than benchmarking, and looks for particular ways your customer service is better or worse than that of specific competitors.

Acceptance Tests are used when building a new automated system to make sure the system will meet project goals. Acceptance criteria, and sometimes even precise test methods, can be written into vendor contracts.

Modifying an Existing System requires testing to make sure the changes will have the desired effect. These tests don't have to be as detailed as acceptance tests, but ignoring them will inevitably lead to application drift.

A **Tune-Up** is intended to find simple ways to improve an existing call center or automated system. Tune-ups usually

involve one or two controlled tests, and can be completed in a matter of weeks.

Exploratory Testing is used to evaluate and refine proto-types of a new IVR or speech recognition system. These tests are small, fast, and inexpensive, giving you the ability to test many different versions of the same application.

Customer Service Auditing

16

Ingredients
- **Monitor Call Stats:** Real-Time or Daily
- **Agent Feedback:** Daily to Weekly
- **Log Analysis:** Weekly to Monthly
- **Controlled Tests:** Monthly to Semi-Annually
- **Survey Past Callers:** Quarterly to Semi-Annually

Just as a financial audit provides rigorous assurance of the accuracy of a company's income statement and balance sheet, a customer service audit is intended to provide detailed information about the performance of a call center, and provide an early warning for service problems. Customer service audits should be an ongoing process, but can also be done on a one-time basis. Audits should be in-depth examinations of your customer service performance, not superficial "feel-good" exercises.

A program of regular audits is like an annual physical for your call center: you do it to make sure everything is really as healthy as you think it is, and to try to find problems that hadn't been noticed before. This is also a good opportunity to look for ways to improve customer service, just as a visit to the doctor is likely to result in a lecture to lose weight or quit smoking.

Each element of the call center is part of a complex system that often includes live agents, automated service, separate channels of communication such as the Internet, and interactions with different branches of the same company. This complex system operates in an environment that also includes customer expectations and history, distractions and noise, and your advertising. Even your competition can affect your customer service: think how many coffee shops had to learn what "double tall" meant when Starbuck's first rolled into town!

The most common problems we find in customer service audits are related to minor updates that turn out to have a major impact. A new message here, a tiny feature added there, and pretty soon it's entirely different from the application that worked when it was first rolled out. *

A classic example is when a company decides to use its marketing vocabulary in an IVR. The first prompt on all the phone systems is changed from: "Welcome to Acme. Press 1 if you are an Acme customer" to "Welcome to Acme. Press 1 if you are an Acme Partner." ** It is easy for everyone inside the company to become so immersed in the vocabulary that nobody realizes customers might get confused.

Audits tell you how well your call center is doing right now, and they detect changes over time. For both goals to be achieved, the auditing program needs to be consistent.

An effective audit program measures performance in many different ways. Each measurement complements the others, and provides a slightly different view of the overall performance. Doing easy tests often—such as

An audit should be:

- Repeated on a regular basis.
- Large enough to provide meaningful data.
- Consistent enough to compare statistics from different reports.

From the audit you should learn:

- How your call center is doing.
- Callers' attitudes toward your call center and your company.
- How callers' attitudes and behavior changes over time.
- The mix of callers and how it changes over time.

You might also learn:

- What information callers want that you don't provide.
- What products and services callers request but you don't sell.

 This assumes the system really did work when it was first rolled out. In some cases, it was never rigorously tested before being deployed.

** In one system where the IVR used marketing jargon in its first menu, 5% of callers got confused and bailed out at the first prompt. One word, trivial as it sounds, was costing a significant amount of money.

monitoring call stats and performing log analysis—serves as a tripwire in case something changes. Gathering data from live callers is more costly and time-consuming, but it is the only way to understand what your callers actually think about your service. Each type of data will raise questions best answered through other means.

Monitor Call Stats

Call stats, such as average call length, daily call volume, IVR abandon rates, and average time on hold, provide relatively little insight into the actual level of service callers are receiving. However, these metrics usually cost almost nothing to generate, and they reflect any change in the performance of the call center almost instantly. This makes them useful as an immediate warning that something needs to be investigated further.

Call stats should be calculated at least daily and graphed to provide context for the normal values, long-term trends, and any sudden changes. Many call centers calculate a few call stats continuously and monitor them in real time. This real time monitoring is a valuable tactical aid, helping agents and managers allocate their time where it is most needed.

You don't need to spend a lot of time analyzing every little blip, but you do want to keep your eyes peeled for both long-term trends and sudden changes. Trend data is extremely helpful for planning, while sudden changes should be noted and possibly investigated.

Agent Feedback

Like monitoring call stats, gathering feedback from call center agents is almost free and should be done frequently. Agents are aware of things in the call center environment to which both managers and computers are blind, and may hear of incidents—such as glitches in the automation—that call stats don't pick up.

Agents also have the ability to provide some interpretation and suggestions for improvement. It is important to keep in mind that agents will be biased about their own performance and don't always see the big picture.

Log Analysis

Log analysis takes a more detailed look at the technical data from a call center, sometimes using statistical techniques and data mining. This analysis should be performed regularly enough to catch trouble spots as they develop. It is useful for identifying where callers have difficulty in an automated system. Prompts with high opt-out or abandon rates, unusually frequent speech recognition errors, and points where callers often go back to the prior menu are all red flags that can be identified through log analysis.

These trouble spots can be related to any number of different issues, ranging from poorly-worded prompts all the way to outright bugs in the automation. If necessary, a controlled test should be used to identify the root cause of the problem and figure out how to fix it.

Controlled Test

Call stats, agent feedback, and log analysis all provide performance data from inside the call center. To get a complete picture of what's happening you will have to step outside the call center and gather data from the caller's perspective.

A controlled test is the preferred vehicle, since it provides the most complete and cost-effective view of the entire customer service interaction: recordings correlated to caller opinions and information about why and how many times each person called.

The other important function of periodic controlled testing is to make sure internal data isn't misleading you into a false sense of security.

We recommend performing a periodic large-scale test with 500 to 1,000 participants split among several different tasks. Some of these tasks will be the same on every test, in order

Find out how we can improve service.

We're looking for ways to improve.

Well, I do have a suggestion...

That shouldn't be hard to change.

I take full credit for improving our customer satisfaction.

to provide a baseline picture of overall performance. Other tasks may change from test to test to focus on specific issues. This regularly scheduled test can be done all at once, or as a trickle over the course of several weeks or months.

If there are issues of immediate concern, you may want to augment regular controlled tests with one or more rapid assessments, since they can provide a snapshot within days or hours.

Data from controlled tests will almost always point the way to making operational improvements in the call center. After changes are made, the next controlled test should include tasks to make sure the changes had the desired impact on performance and satisfaction.

Survey Past Callers

Surveying past callers is one of the only ways to discover what actual paying customers think of your call center. Unfortunately, it is limited in its ability to turn those opinions into actionable changes in the call center, and can be expensive to do on a large scale.

We recommend surveying past callers as a reality check on all the other audit methods, particularly controlled tests. As a reality check, it needs to be done on a large enough scale to gather statistically meaningful data (400-500 responses), but not as often as the other techniques. It is also important to make sure your survey method is reasonably free of bias.

You should expect the survey of past callers to provide data about the overall satisfaction level of your call center. This should track with satisfaction data from the controlled tests, but won't match exactly due to statistical biases and errors in both tests.

Recipe Variation: One-Time Audit

Sometimes there isn't the budget or institutional motivation for an ongoing audit program, but you want to get a general sense of how your call center is performing. Or you may suspect that you have a problem, and need to pin it down and find out how to fix it. In this case, you want to do a one-time audit.

A one-time audit is similar to an ongoing audit program, but smaller in scope and not designed to be repeated, though it has the potential to evolve into an ongoing audit program.

Two of the tests from an ongoing audit program don't make sense as part of a one-time audit: monitoring call stats doesn't provide any useful data if it isn't repeated;✱ and surveying past callers has limited value for finding specific problems and action items.

Agent Feedback and Log Analysis

These steps need to be done first, to provide data about potential problems spots and direction for the controlled tests. You should be looking to answer questions like *What kind of complaints are we getting?* and *Where is the automated system performing worse than expected?*

✱ You should be monitoring call stats even if you don't have an ongoing audit program. We just don't consider it part of a one-time audit.

This will generate working theories about where the trouble spots are, and you may be able to fix the more blatant problems at this stage.

Controlled Test

Once you've gathered data from inside the call center, and have some idea of where the problem areas are, perform a controlled test. This test should be focused more on specific problems, and less on measuring the overall call center performance.

Audit Pitfalls

The biggest problems around an audit are not making a concerted effort to find problems, and not making use of the data effectively.

The purpose of an audit program is to make sure the call center is performing properly and provide early warning of problems. It can be tempting to unconsciously craft the audit program in a way that minimizes any bad news. This can happen through discouraging honest feedback from agents, poorly-worded survey questions, and not making an effort to follow up on identified potential problems. It is also tempting to include meaningless feel-good questions on surveys.✱ This temptation needs to be resisted, since deluding oneself or management about the quality of your customer service will only hurt in the long run.

Once you've identified problems and potential solutions, it is important to implement the solutions—or for more complex problems, do a cost-benefit analysis to find out whether it makes sense to fix the problem. Without the step of fixing problems, the purpose of the audit is defeated. Data that sits on the shelf does nobody any good.

✱ A "meaningless feel-good" question is one that asks callers how they felt without providing any context or historical data. Opinion questions have very strong biases, and without some sort of context you can't tell whether your results are good or bad.

70

17 Benchmarking

A benchmark is less thorough than an audit, and is intended to compare a call center's performance to industry norms, another call center, or the same call center at a different time. Benchmarks are best if they measure something related to the goals of the call center, and do it on a meaningful scale. To be useful, benchmarks must be measured and calculated in a completely consistent fashion, and with enough data to have reasonable statistical accuracy.

Benchmarks can be constructed using any ingredient that generates numerical data, such as controlled studies, follow-up surveys, call stats, statistics gathered from log analysis, and numerical scores generated from call recordings. The only methods that can't be used are ones like rules of thumb, which provide only subjective results.

Consistency is the bane of many attempts to benchmark call center performance. Even slight changes to the data collection method can dramatically change the results, and many people use different definitions for "industry standard" metrics. If you are using a third party to supply benchmarks, you need be careful that the data you buy is high quality and internally consistent.

Building a Benchmark in Four Steps

1. Decide what you want to know

The most important step in building a benchmark is to decide what you want to measure. Normally, this will be related to a business goal of the call center, such as caller satisfaction, customer retention, operational cost, or revenue. Sometimes this can be directly measured, but more often it has to be calculated from other information that is a proxy for the business goal.

2. Create a numerical score that measures what you want to know

Once you know what you want to benchmark, you need to find a way to express it numerically. There may be many different ways to calculate the same number, and it is more important to always calculate the benchmark the same way than to find the "ideal" way to calculate it.

3. Gather data and calculate benchmark score

The details of gathering data and calculating the score may be determined for you if you use an outside vendor for benchmarking. Often, the vendor will already have a database of historical benchmarks, and if you want to compare your performance to the historical data, you need to be completely consistent. ✱

✱ A good benchmarking service will insist that all clients measure the benchmarks in exactly the same way. While it can be very hard to tell a client "no" when they have their own way of doing things, inconsistent benchmarks are useless.

If you're building a new benchmark from scratch, then you have considerable freedom in how to measure the data and calculate the benchmark score. You should focus on making sure that the data you are using in the benchmark is data you can gather easily and consistently, and that what you measure really reflects what you think it will measure. As you get going, you may want to try several different ways to calculate the benchmark score to see how sensitive it is to the details of your formula.

4. Make comparisons and determine a course of action

Finally, the entire purpose of a benchmark is to allow comparisons between your customer service and something else. If you intend to compare your operation to a competitor or industry norms, you will be forced to use a third party to provide your benchmarks. It is important that your vendor provide not just the benchmark data itself, but an explanation of how the data was gathered, and what the relevance of your score is.

Benchmark Pitfalls

Benchmarking is one of the most common reasons for measuring call center performance. Unfortunately, if a benchmark isn't done properly it becomes misleading or useless, and the traps can be subtle.

One of the most common pitfalls is a naïve benchmark, when a particular measurement is assumed to mean something it doesn't. For example, call time is sometimes used to measure call quality: the assumption is that longer calls indicate inefficient agents or confused and irritated callers. In reality, there can be many reasons for long calls, including complex transactions and lots

Example Satisfaction Benchmark

One benchmark we frequently use is based on a standard survey question we ask on nearly all our studies: *How satisfied were you with your overall experience?* Participants are given five options from "Very Satisfied" to "Very Dissatisfied."

The raw benchmark score is calculated by subtracting the percent of callers who were "Dissatisfied" or "Very Dissatisfied" from the percent of callers who were "Very Satisfied." The score can hypothetically range from −100 (everyone was dissatisfied) to +100 (everyone was very satisfied).

To make the benchmark more intuitive, we express it as a letter grade from "A" to "D." The letter grades are based on a curve, where the best 25% of systems we test get an "A", the next best get a "B" and so forth down to "D" which is the worst 25% of systems we test.

When we were creating this benchmark, we tried calculating the raw score a number of different ways, but found that the letter grades usually didn't change for any reasonable formula. As a result we consider this benchmark robust.

of upselling; while inefficient agents may transfer or hang up to improve their statistics.

Especially when it comes to measuring something as fuzzy as satisfaction, making the wrong measurement can be misleading.✱ As described in Appendix A, *Nobody Reads an Appendix on Statistics*, even the right question can be wrong if you systematically ignore certain people. It may be better to choose multiple measurements and combine them, rather than to rely on a single indicator.

✱ Worse, the concept of "satisfaction" is subjective, and we find that callers and companies often have different ideas about what it means. To the company, a "satisfied" customer is considered a positive outcome, but we find that customers who call themselves "satisfied" are often ambivalent about the experience. To them, being "satisfied" means that the company met, but did not exceed, expectations.

Inconsistency is another common problem in benchmarking, usually because a consultant or vendor takes shortcuts when gathering a benchmark database. When the benchmark database isn't reliable, any comparisons to the database are meaningless. Valid benchmarking

Congratulations!
My benchmark shows you're
in the top 15% of all
airline call centers!

Good work. Everyone
in customer service gets
a bonus this month.

Should I point out we're a
bank, not an airline?

requires all the data to be gathered and calculated in precisely the same way. Some vendors use self-reported data from call centers in their database, which is not only guaranteed to be inconsistent, but call centers have an incentive to report good numbers to make themselves look better.

Too much precision is another common benchmarking pitfall. Benchmark results should be either expressed with a margin of error, or in increments that are statistically meaningful. For example, if a benchmark scale runs from 1 to 10, then a one-unit change should be larger than the benchmark's margin of error. Otherwise, one month a call center might score an 8 and the next month a 7, leading to a great deal of hair-pulling and lost bonuses even if the change is due to random error or events that make no real difference. In this example, a scale from 1 to 5 may be more appropriate.

Competitive Analysis

Ingredients
- **Audit or Benchmark Results** of your own call center
- **Controlled Test** of your competition

In retail stores, it's common practice to have mystery shoppers check on the competition's service and prices. A similar thing can be done for customer service by using controlled tests of other companies. This can be done without the knowledge of the companies you're testing, since it is just a systematic way of calling their published customer service numbers and finding out how they handle the calls.

Competitive analysis is straightforward. You may be able to use existing data from your internal benchmarking and auditing (see Chapter 16, *Customer Service Auditing*, and Chapter 17, *Benchmarking*) and collect similar statistics on the competition. In some industries, such as banking or cell phone customer service, it may be necessary to recruit your competitor's customers as study participants, but a good research firm will have this capability.

When you do competitive analysis, be sure to analyze your own call center at the same time in the same way.

Competitive Analysis Pitfalls

The two biggest pitfalls to competitive analysis are not paying enough attention, and paying too much attention to the results.

At one extreme, it is tempting to find reasons and excuses for why a competitor is doing better than you: "They don't have as big of a turnover problem," "They've got more budget than we do," and so forth. Or, if your customer service is better than the competition, you may dismiss everything they do and not recognize good ideas they've implemented.

At the other extreme you may find yourself blindly imitating everything the competition does, especially if you're losing business. This can be dangerous: there may be reasons why what they're doing won't work for you, and it is disruptive to make big changes every time someone comes up with a new idea.

You want to steer the middle ground: use the competitive analysis as a way to get new ideas and set realistic goals for your own customer service operation.

Acceptance
Testing

Ingredients
- **Automated Load Test**
- **Traversal Test**
- **Large Scale Test**
- **Pilot Test**

Before any new automated system is implemented it needs to pass a series of acceptance tests. Ideally, these are written into the contract with the vendor or consultant building the new system. Acceptance criteria should cover both the technical functionality of the system (i.e. can it handle the expected call volume) and the design functionality of the interface (i.e. can callers figure out how to use it). Typically, the vendor has numerical targets it must meet, often with penalties for nonperformance.

The goal of an acceptance test is to shake down a system that is nearly ready to be deployed, and confirm that it meets performance targets. Acceptance tests should be objective and statistically meaningful so there is little room for argument about suc-

An acceptance test should be:

- Extensive and realistic enough to accurately predict how the application will perform in the real world.

From the test you should learn:

- What flaws need to be fixed before it can be deployed.
- Whether or not the system has met all the criteria necessary for deployment.
- How well it should perform once it is deployed.

cess. Many acceptance criteria are technical, such as the number of simultaneous calls an IVR can handle, or the average call time to complete a particular task. Controlled tests make it possible to also set targets for ease of use, caller satisfaction, and task completion.

Acceptance tests are often part of a contract with third-party developers. A good set of acceptance criteria is one of the most important factors in project success, since the developers have a strong motivation to meet their contractual targets.

The worst case is when the contract spells out detailed implementation specifications, but not what callers are supposed to be able to accomplish. For example, a call flow diagram is part of the contract, but there is no requirement that callers will be successful at using the IVR. If the specified design doesn't work, the contract doesn't allow a useful system to be delivered—a bad situation for the everyone involved. Instead, write contracts to specify usability targets and leave implementation details out.

Acceptance Criteria

The purpose of an acceptance test is to make sure the system meets the acceptance criteria, which are often negotiated in advance between the company and the vendor. Acceptance criteria can set targets for both the technical performance and the usability of the system. For example, an airline deploying a new automated information line might negotiate these acceptance criteria:

Technical Criteria

- The system can handle 480 simultaneous calls without performance degradation.

- 99.9% of calls will be answered by the system within five seconds.

Usability Criteria

- 90% of callers who know a flight's arrival city, departure city, and departure time can find out the arrival time in one call without talking to a live agent.

- 85% of callers report being "very satisfied" with the experience.

Automated Load Test

Load tests are very common in acceptance testing. They make sure the system won't break or slow down when subjected to a large volume of calls. There are a number of testing labs that provide this service, and many larger vendors perform load testing in-house.

The test regimen normally includes many different call paths to ensure that the entire application is tested. In addition to measuring whether or not the system fails, calls may be timed to make sure that there are no unacceptable pauses or delays when the system is heavily loaded.

The load test should represent the worst-case scenario the system is expected to encounter in the real world, in terms of simultaneous calls, processing load, database load, and any other factors that may affect performance. This is particularly critical with speech recognition systems, where the processing load on the speech recognition engine can vary widely throughout the application.

Traversal Test

A traversal test will verify that the system was built the way it was designed. It uncovers places where the wrong recording was used, where two recordings don't sound right when played together, or where the application fails to work entirely. It can find rare but catastrophic bugs that may not show up in other kinds of tests.

To do a traversal test, engineers or testers call into the system and run through scripts that hit each entry and exit point of each dialog at least once. This is not the same as a usability test since it does not gather opinions of outside callers.

Large Scale Test

Where the combination of an automated stress test and a traversal test tells you whether or not a system will perform as designed, there is only one way to test whether or not the VUI was properly designed. A large (500 participants or more) controlled test needs to be used, with individual callers being given scenarios representing tasks the system is designed to handle.

It is important to get data representing the performance of the application as a whole, and also to exercise all of the most important paths through the system. Choose scenarios to provide the most realistic measure of the system's performance.

Finally, it is important to use participants who are a reasonable reflection of the actual people who are expected to call the application after it is deployed. Employees of the vendor and employees of the company buying the system are not realistic callers (in most cases), and should not be used.

Pilot Test

Many companies test their new systems using a phased roll-out, or pilot test. A percentage of live customer calls are sent to the new system, and call recordings are analyzed for any problems. This can provide useful information when done in conjunction with the techniques described above, but it is best to think of this as a deployment strategy rather than a testing strategy. You want to be confident that the system will work as intended before using paying customers as unwitting guinea pigs.

Because it deals with real callers and real situations, a pilot test provides information that controlled tests cannot, such as an unexpected mix of callers or people trying to use the system for unexpected things. Unfortunately, that information often falls in the "too little, too late" category: if people are calling for reasons you didn't anticipate, you usually can't add functionality at the last minute. If you did your homework when you designed the system, controlled tests should reflect actual usage.

A pilot test will help uncover transition or integration problems that occur as the new system is fully deployed. But by the time you get to the pilot you should be confident that the system itself works.

Acceptance Test Pitfalls

The biggest pitfall in acceptance testing is simply not doing it. Acceptance testing comes late in a project cycle, when both time and money are often in short supply. There can be a lot of pressure to deploy now, and clean up the mess later. Unfortunately, the cleanup from a hastily deployed application can be far more expensive and time-consuming than even the most rigorous of acceptance test regimens.

Another major pitfall is not agreeing ahead of time with the vendor on acceptance criteria and testing methodology. Vendors have a strong incentive to make sure their systems pass acceptance tests. If everyone agrees in advance what the tests will be, a smart vendor will incorporate preliminary testing into the project timeline, resulting in a better system and a project that is more likely to be on time and on budget.

Finally, when an acceptance test discovers a problem, there may be little time or money left to fix it. Companies will sometimes go ahead and deploy a system they know is broken simply because there is no other option.

 The authors are aware of several very large call center applications that were prematurely deployed. One cost over a million dollars to develop, and was completely disconnected weeks after being deployed due to customer complaints. Another is still in service, but after almost two years is still not performing even close to an acceptable level.

20 Modifying an Existing Automated System

Ingredients
- **Audit** or **Benchmark** Results
- **Controlled Test**
- **Traversal Test**

Even small changes can have a big effect on how callers use your IVR or speech recognition system. For example, using industry-specific jargon at an important prompt can make the system dramatically harder to use. Any time you change an existing system you should be on the lookout for unintended consequences.

Audit or Benchmark Results

Before modifying an automated system you should determine its performance (see Chapter 16, *Customer Service Auditing* and Chapter 17, *Benchmarking*) so you will be able to measure any impact the change had. You can use data from a regular audit, or include a mini-audit or benchmark study in the early stages of designing the change.

Controlled Test

In simple cases, you only need to compare the results from a "before and after" test that shows the change in performance as a result of the modification. If you have a regular auditing program in place, both tests can be part of the ongoing test program and won't cost anything more than what you're already spending. This "before and after" testing will tell you if the changes had the desired effect, or if you need to go back to the drawing board.

For large changes there should be a baseline audit followed by an acceptance test. This is appropriate for changes that are expected to have a significant impact on customer service and call center performance.

Traversal Test

Once you have made your changes, a mini traversal test is necessary to uncover subtle bugs or ugly juxtapositions of recordings. It doesn't have to test the entire application, but you need to check every part of the system that the change will impact.

Modifying an Existing System Pitfalls

The biggest pitfall is doing no testing of changes at all. We know that small changes sometimes have a big impact, but some call centers will cheerfully change prompts, menu options, and even speech recognition grammars without doing any testing. This leads to application drift.

Application drift is when an automated system performs well when first implemented, but over the course of months or years gradually gets worse and worse. Some companies blame the vendor when this happens, but the real culprit is the gradual accumulation of small changes that when taken together make the system incoherent, confusing, or even completely broken. Call center systems can also drift as customers' expectations change (for example, as a result of a marketing campaign), which is why an ongoing auditing program is also important.

Tune-Up

Ingredients
- **Rapid Assessment**
- **Large-Scale Test**

To make sure you are getting the most out of your call center, it's a good idea to regularly evaluate it. As we discussed in Chapter 16, *Customer Service Auditing*, you can't just assume that a call center will keep running the same way forever, even if it is fully automated. Minor changes can have major impacts, and callers' expectations change over time.

We recommend creating a regular auditing program, but that's not always within the budget or will of every call center. If you have limited time or budget, and want to find some quick ways to improve your performance, a Tune-Up is called for.

There are two approaches: the rapid assessment, or the large scale test. A rapid assessment is fast, inexpensive, and somewhat cursory. A

A Tune-Up should be:

- Large enough to discover most problems
- As realistic as possible

From the test you should learn:

- What simple changes you can make that will improve your call center or IVR performance
- What larger projects might be worth exploring

large scale test will be far more complete, and can also be used to benchmark your performance.

Rapid Assessment

A rapid assessment will involve having a few dozen people call your call center over the course of an hour or two, try a typical task, and report back any problems they encountered. When these reports are matched to call recordings, a picture of what went wrong develops, and often leads directly to solutions.

This is most appropriate when you already have some idea of what problems you have in your call center. For example, if you have a lot of people hanging up when trying to transfer money from one account to another, you can focus your test on that particular task.

Large Scale Test

A large scale test gives you the opportunity to explore more areas of your call center, do benchmarking, and cast a wider net for problems. A large study can take from a few days to a few weeks, and can involve hundreds or thousands of participants.

This is most appropriate when you don't want to limit your testing to one particular task, when you want to be able to quantify your overall performance, or when you're looking for more subtle problems.

Tune-Up Pitfalls

The whole point of a tune-up is to find simple ways to improve your customer service. It can be tempting to look at the results and think that a complete overhaul is needed (which might be true), but such major changes are not the point of a tune-up. Focus on the short-term return on investment, but use the data from the tune-up as a launching pad when the opportunity for more significant changes presents itself.

Exploratory Testing

Ingredients
- **Application Prototype**
- **Controlled Test**

The worst time to discover a problem is when it's too late to do anything about it. Unfortunately, that's exactly when the most intensive testing of new call center systems occurs.

An exploratory test should be:

- Quick and inexpensive, so you can re-design and re-test.
- Accurate enough to be useful— and not misleading!

From the test you should learn:

- Whether or not a general design has major flaws
- Which design elements befuddle callers
- Which elements look complicated on paper but callers take in stride.

Exploratory tests, on the other hand, are done primarily on prototypes of new projects before design decisions have been set in stone. Tests are repeated on revised prototypes until the designers are confident that their ideas will work in the real world.

By testing early and often, you can fix flaws in the design of a system before you are too committed to the concept. Testing at this phase is a balancing act between time, expense, and value. If the application is complex or novel, or if the demographics of the callers are unusual, a more intensive testing program is needed.

When in doubt, more testing is almost always cheaper than fixing problems after the system is mostly finished.

Testing a prototype is much different from testing later on. For one thing, it is understood that the final system is likely to be quite different from the early prototypes. For another, you will want the flexibility to do multiple tests, in case the first few ideas turn out to be disasters. The goal is not to get little ideas for tweaking (though it does happen), but rather to avert disasters before they become expensive to fix. Exploratory tests will occasionally even lead you to start over from scratch.

The key to exploratory tests is to do them quickly and cheaply so that doing one more test and one more redesign isn't a burden. It is best to use a test-redesign-retest cycle, rather than testing several ideas in parallel, since even radically different prototypes can fail in the same way because of a common blind spot in the design.

Application Prototype

You should plan to build and test several different prototypes, since fixing one problem may introduce others. This implies fast, flexible and inexpensive testing. It is also important to get the prototype as similar to the real thing as possible. There's no magic bullet here, since speed and accuracy are contradictory goals (see Chapter 5, *Prototyping*).

When possible, a working prototype will make for a more realistic test, and has the advantage of being easier to use with modern testing techniques like the rapid assessment. In some cases a Wizard of Oz (WOZ) prototype is the only way to go, either because of the complexity of the application, or the capabilities of the team building the prototype.

Many developers of speech recognition applications swear by WOZ testing and wouldn't think of designing any VUI without it. Others are equally passionate that it's too much effort and expense for too little value, so they don't do any exploratory testing at all. The problem with WOZ isn't the style of prototype, but the cost and time burdens imposed by a traditional lab test.

Controlled Test

The other key element in exploratory testing is gathering data, usually through either a lab test or a rapid assessment. Lab tests have the advantage of being able to give more attention to each participant—including careful screening and being able to ask detailed questions about things that happened in a particular call.

Rapid assessments are much more efficient, though they don't provide as much data on individual participants. Where the practical limit of lab testing seems to be about a dozen participants, rapid assessments can easily include over a hundred participants at significantly lower cost than even a small lab test.

The more appropriate test method depends primarily on how narrow your target demographic is. If the general public is a reasonable proxy for your callers, the rapid assessment is the way to go. But if you need to make sure the application works for neurologists who speak fluent Estonian, recruiting individual test participants for a more intensive study may be the only option.

Exploratory Test Pitfalls

By their nature, exploratory tests are small. As a result, when a problem only affects one or two participants, it is tempting to write it off as a fluke. The opposite is actually closer to the truth: because these tests are so small, any problem experienced by any participant is likely to be a significant problem in the real world.

The other major pitfall is doing only one or two exploratory tests. The whole point of having small, inexpensive tests is to allow many tests over the course of a project cycle. One exploratory test will give valuable data, but only in a limited and narrow sense. Testing should be sprinkled throughout the design process, both to validate changes and to look for new problems.

Gourmet Meal Planning: The Life of an Automated System

Now that we've discussed the concepts behind a scientific approach to customer service, introduced the basic techniques for measuring customer service performance, and provided a number of scenarios and appropriate test regimens for each, it is time to assemble everything into a complete view of how to use data and measurement to provide gourmet customer service. We'll use the example of a company building, deploying, and operating an automated customer service system, since this is very common in modern call centers.

From a testing perspective, the life of an automated system is like a meal. We have the ingredients, which are different test methods and concepts. We assemble the ingredients into recipes, which are the kinds of testing we use in various situations. Finally, we have to assemble those recipes in a way that will ensure that the system performs as well as possible within the budget and time allowed. Simple systems are like a picnic or backyard barbecue, while a large and complex application may demand a testing regimen like an eight-course gourmet extravaganza.

How you approach the development of a new system depends on several factors including the process your development team is most comfortable with and your tolerance for risk. Risk factors include:

- The cost of service interruptions. Everybody says that downtime is unacceptable, but in some cases that's just talk. In other cases minutes of downtime can be measured in thousands of dollars or, in the case of emergency response systems, lives lost.

- The cost of a marginally useful, misleading, embarrassing, or annoying system. For example, callers never get a critical piece of information or the Spanish translation contains an embarrassing mistake.

- How quickly and easily you will be able to fix mistakes after the system is deployed, while ensuring that the fix doesn't introduce new bugs. This is a major issue in many

companies, since once the project is "complete," it may be difficult to get the budget even for small, obvious fixes.

- How quickly you can detect problems in a running system. Down time is easy to detect, but a faux pas depends on someone telling you about it. How often do you talk to customers? Is your development team in the know, or are they usually the last to hear the latest company rumor?

For low-risk systems, an agile development methodology may be appropriate if the development team is comfortable with that approach (see Appendix B, *Usability Testing and Agile Software Development*). Under agile development, the development team cycles through project phases several times, each time producing a more sophisticated application. For mission critical applications, a write-once-and-test-to-death approach may be necessary, and with contingency plans in place in case all that testing is ultimately not good enough.

Regardless of what you decide to do, most projects have six phases, and each phase will go faster and smoother with the appropriate testing. The longer and more formalized each phase, the more testing is needed at each step.

Even though the six phases happen sequentially, the order is not set in stone. For example, suppose the VUI designers assumed a particular database query wouldn't take much time, but the actual query takes several seconds. The result can be software that works great when using a test database, but has long, awkward pauses when plugged into the real database. To fix it, the system needs to be redesigned and re-coded—which could take minutes, but it could also take days or weeks. Reality can be a lot messier than the project diagrams and theories of software development would have you believe.

Analysis Phase

During this phase of development, you are primarily gathering information that will allow you to design your new system. This is where you get to know the callers, including who calls, how often, and why. It's also important to audit your current call center so you can set appropriate project goals. For example, if most callers are annoyed with your company when they pick up the phone, a target of 80% of them being thrilled with your IVR may be unrealistic. Auditing will also give you the data you need at the end of the project to find out if the application made your service better, and if so, how much better.

This is also a good time to do competitive analysis. By seeing what your competitors do, you can get some ideas for your application—either copying their ideas or intentionally differentiating yourself. By seeing how well they do, you'll know how hard you'll need to work in order to be better.

Project Testing Menu

Phase	Description	Tests
Analysis	Evaluate what you already have and what you need. This is when you ask questions like "who are my callers?" Also known as requirements phase.	Auditing Benchmarking Competitive analysis
Design	Scope out what you plan to develop in greater detail. This is when you ask how callers will react to a particular design idea.	Exploratory tests
Code	Go from a design to working software.	
Test	You're somewhat confident in both the design and implementation, but you need to make certain that it's ready to be deployed and that it works in the production environment.	Acceptance tests
Release	The software is rolled out and starts to handle real calls.	Pilot test
Operations	The system is fully operational and handling live calls. This is sometimes called the maintenance phase, since changes are usually limited to bug fixes and updates.	Auditing Benchmarking Competitive Analysis

Project goals are also defined here, making it the best time to design the tests that will be used throughout the rest of the project. Similar test designs can be used for exploratory testing, acceptance tests, and audits. Test specifications—both technical and caller-focused—are a good way to communicate project requirements.

The test design is a description of test methodology, the goal of the test, and the data you will collect. While test designs can't communicate every requirement, they can describe many project requirements in an unambiguous and measurable way.

Design Phase

The design phase is where exploratory testing gets done. Prototypes are designed and tested, and the lessons from the test are applied to new prototypes. This continues until the design is good enough.

The wrong way to go about design is to focus on flowcharts and call flow diagrams. Seasoned professionals can read a call flow and have some sense of how good it will be, but many others won't be able to make the conceptual leap from diagram to how the system will actually sound.

Rather, design should be focused on prototypes, with the prototype as the design, rather than the paper diagram as the design. That ensures everyone will have the same idea of how the system will work, and that the design has been tested in the most realistic way possible. Using iterative testing of prototypes will lead to a much better final design than what can be done on paper.

Coding Phase

Seasoned software developers will use a variety of software tests as they write the code, though these tests normally address the internal functioning of the software and not issues like usability. As a practical matter, diligent testing in this phase results in bugs getting fixed quickly, which leads to a smoother test phase and fewer surprises.

Test Phase

After the application has been programmed comes the test phase. Testing has been going on since the beginning of the project, but this is where it is most intensive. This is also your last chance to find and fix problems before inflicting them on paying customers. For mission-critical systems, tests can take weeks to set up and run.

Many acceptance tests are technical, but usability is often more important. We frequently see systems that are well-built and meet the technical requirements of the customer, but for whatever reason, a large percentage of callers can't or won't use it. That's why we recommend that the project specification includes usability requirements, and those requirements are tested at this phase.

Operational Phase

Once a system is fully operational, testing will mostly be auditing and benchmarking. Chapter 16, *Customer Service Auditing*, and Chapter 17, *Benchmarking*, discuss auditing and benchmarking in depth, but there are a few points that bear repeating. Minor changes can have a major impact. Changing a single word in a single prompt can cause confusion, if you go from plain English to marketing-speak, or if you forgot that the same recording is re-used in a different part of the system. Don't let familiarity blind you to how your customer service appears to your customers!

Appendices

Nobody Reads an Appendix on Statistics

Understanding how to measure the quality of customer service requires at least a basic understanding of the most important tool: statistics. Knowledge of statistics is as important to gourmet customer service as knowledge of slicing, mixing, and baking is to a gourmet chef. A complete overview of statistics is well beyond what we can provide in this short book, but some basic statistical knowledge and a few rules of thumb are enough to avoid the most common traps.

The science of statistics is the science of imprecision. In the call center, statistics helps you answer three key questions: *Can you trust the data you are gathering about your call center? Will the data tell you what you need to know?* and *Do you have enough data?*

Statistics takes incomplete, inaccurate data about the world and tries to draw conclusions from it. It would be wonderful and amazing

Most readers will probably have at least some familiarity with basic statistical terms and concepts, though we won't assume any particular knowledge. For those who want more background in a highly readable and entertaining format, we recommend *The Cartoon Guide to Statistics*, by Larry Gonick and Woollcott Smith.

if we could somehow gather complete and accurate data about, for example, caller satisfaction. But in the real world, we can't afford to be 100% complete, and it isn't possible to be 100% accurate.✱

So in the real world, we use statistics to understand just how good (or bad) the data is, and whether or not we can rely on the results.

There are two main reasons why data might not be reliable: because it is imprecise, leading to *error*; or because something about the way the data is being collected leads to a systematic *bias*.

Error and Bias

Take a simple survey: Three Point Mortgage is a national financial services company. Recently, Three Point Mortgage has been losing market share, and management thinks it may be because of poor customer service in the call center. The company embarks upon a program to measure its customer satisfaction and look for ways to improve its call center. To do this, Three Point Mortgage will survey callers to find out how satisfied they are and what Three Point can do to improve.

Question Bias

The first problem the company faces is that there are many different ways to ask the same question. While different questions may appear to be asking the same thing, each one will

---

Satisfaction Questions

There are many different ways to ask about satisfaction. Each of these questions has a different bias, making it impossible to compare survey results using one question to results using a different question.

On a scale of 1 to 10, with "1" being the worst and "10" being the best, how satisfied were you with how your call to Three Point Mortgage was handled?

Please mark the point on the line that corresponds to your satisfaction with Three Point Mortgage:

Very Satisfied   Very Dissatisfied

Please circle the face that best describes your experience calling Three Point Mortgage:

How satisfied or dissatisfied were you with your overall experience calling Three Point Mortgage?

- ☐ Very Satisfied
- ☐ Satisfied
- ☐ Neither Satisfied nor Dissatisfied
- ☐ Dissatisfied
- ☐ Very Dissatisfied

produce different results, since each question is differently biased. In fact, not only is it hard to write "unbiased" questions about people's opinions, in some cases it's hard to even know what "unbiased" means.

As a rule of thumb, factual questions tend to be relatively unbiased, but questions about opinions or hypothetical situations have strong biases. Certain types of questions tend to be biased as well: most people will say that they are "satisfied" with a company even if they are ambivalent, and people tend to report having a more positive experience than what a neutral observer would conclude.

 A "complete" survey would get a response from 100% of the people in the group of interest, i.e. 100% of customers or 100% of employees. An "accurate" survey, in contrast, measures precisely the data you want to measure. Given that concepts like "satisfaction" and "quality" are fuzzy to begin with, it isn't easy to write a survey that collects exactly the data you want.

Even the order questions are asked can change the answers people give. Questions should be asked in a logical order, so participants don't have to change mental gears, and possible answers should also be grouped logically. If pos-

---

Reducing Question Bias

- Where possible, ask about facts and past behavior, rather than opinions and future behavior. Example: "Have you purchased from BigRetail in the last 12 months?" instead of "How likely are you to buy from BigRetail in the next year?"

- Group questions logically, i.e. with all demographic questions together, and related opinion questions together. This improves accurate recall.

- Include both extremes in the question. Example: "How Satisfied or Dissatisfied are you?" instead of "How Satisfied are you?"

- If there is no logical order to possible answers, present the choices in a different order to different participants. People are more likely to choose the first and last options in a list.

- As often as possible, reuse questions in exactly the same form between different surveys. This will provide a baseline for comparison.

- Administer surveys in a written form, rather than verbally. This reduces the desire to please the person asking the questions.

Suppose on a survey you first ask the question, "How much do you like to eat cookies?" immediately followed by "How much do you like to drink milk?" The fact that many people associate milk and cookies (and find the combination yummy) will lead to more people saying they like to drink milk than you would get if you asked about milk without first asking about cookies.

sible, don't ask questions where one question might influence the thought process for answering another.*

People will try to please whomever is administering the survey. If a survey is being given by a person, then she or he must not express any preference for one answer over another. It is preferable to administer a survey in writing, but even then the questions must be worded in a way that doesn't favor one answer over another.

It may sound like there's no way to accurately measure opinions, but we can still get useful data even from badly biased questions. The key is to measure opinions in a relative way, rather than in an absolute way. Don't do the survey just once, repeat it, and compare different measurements to each other and to meaningful benchmarks.

Selection Bias

Once Three Point Mortgage has decided what to ask, they need to figure out whom to ask and when. This introduces selection bias, the systematic exclusion or inclusion of some people in the survey.

For example, an online survey will exclude anyone without Internet access; while a phone-based survey will exclude most people who use an answering machine to screen calls. Worst of all, a survey administered at the end of a phone call will exclude anyone who hangs up out of anger or frustration (see Chapter 9, *End Of Call Surveys*).

Even though selection bias is unavoidable, its importance depends on the nature of the bias and the purpose of the survey. If Three Point Mortgage knows that its customers are 50% men and 50% women, but 75% of survey respondents are women, then there is a clear bias. This may not matter if men and women tend to answer the survey questions in the same way. If men and women give very different answers, the survey will give misleading results. It could, for example, show that satisfaction is increasing, when the reality is that among all customers the satisfaction level is going down.

Selection bias will be most important when trying to make accurate predictions about the behavior of an entire population, and when groups of the population have significantly different opinions or behaviors. For example, polls to predict the outcome of elections are notorious for having bias problems.

Dealing with selection bias comes down to answering one question: *Does the bias matter?* Selection bias will always be present, unless you manage to get nearly 100% of the population to answer the survey. But depending on the nature of the bias and the purpose of the study, the bias might or might not matter.

This is possible for very small groups. For example, if your company only has 100 customers, you may well get 90 of them to respond to a survey. In this fortunate circumstance, the margin of error will also be very small.

One important check is examining the data for anomalies and whether or not they affect the results. For example, if you know that 20% of your customers have an income over $100,000/year, but only 10% of survey respondents fall in that category,

Survey Method	Sources of Selection Bias
Administer survey at the end of a call	• Customers who have a bad call are likely to hang up before the survey. • Customers with negative opinions may refuse to participate.
Follow-up call at a later time	• Customers with strong feelings are more inclined to take the survey. • Certain types of callers are harder to contact by phone.
"Mystery Shoppers" call expressly for evaluation purposes	• Demographics might not match customer population. • Call center agents or "professional survey takers" have a different perspective than customers.

you should check to see if the affluent group gave significantly different responses than the rest of the population. If they answered the same, then you can breathe easy. Otherwise, you may need to take the data with a grain of salt, or even correct it.✱

✱ There are statistical techniques for correcting known biases, but those are well beyond what a typical call center needs to do. Since corrections are tricky and can introduce errors of their own, this is something best left to a professional statistician. Simply being aware of the problem puts you well ahead of the curve.

Another common source of selection bias is self-selection: those who are most motivated to respond are those with the strongest opinions. Unfortunately, there is no way to know what people who *didn't* take the survey would have said. The best way to reduce this bias is to recruit the caller for the survey before the call begins (for example, by asking some of your customers to be part of an ongoing satisfaction study, or by using a "mystery shopper" technique). You can also administer the survey through multiple methods, since some people are more likely to respond to some methods than others.

Selection bias is a fact of life. Like question bias, it cannot be eliminated, merely contained. The best approach is to be aware of it, understand where it is coming from, and try to

---

Coping With Selection Bias

- Look for differences between the survey participants and the population as a whole (for example, in demographic profile). Check to see if underrepresented groups answer survey questions differently than overrepresented groups.

- When possible, recruit the caller for the survey at the beginning of a call, or even before the call; then follow up to make sure the caller actually completes the survey.

- **Don't administer surveys during the call itself**, since callers with the worst experiences will often hang up before getting to the survey. If you must use this technique, **you must make an effort to contact the people who hung up before the end of the call**.

- Where possible, administer the survey in multiple formats. For example, if you do phone-based surveys, also send out E-mail.

structure the study so that the bias won't prevent you from achieving your objective.

Sample Error, aka Margin of Error

Once Three Point Mortgage has settled on a survey design, and has a handle on where they expect to see biases, the next step is to decide how large a survey to run. In a perfect world, Three Point Mortgage would survey every single caller to its call center, but that isn't possible. Since they can afford only a limited number of surveys, the results will be imprecise. The degree of imprecision is the sample error, and is usually expressed as the margin of error.

★★ Suppose you surveyed 2,500 customers and found that 38% of them prefer to drive Japanese cars. In this case the sample error is about 2%, which means if you could have surveyed all of your customers, there's about a 95% chance that between 36% and 40% prefer to drive Japanese cars.

Sample error occurs inevitably when a survey takes a random sample of a group. It is different from selection bias in that sample error is not systematic. Sample error happens because the survey happened to include Joe instead of Bob. Sample error gets smaller when the survey is bigger because the impact of individual survey answers is less important.

The rule of thumb for sample error is that the margin of error is halved when you quadruple the number of survey participants. Surveying 400 people gives a margin of error of about 5%, and you need 1,600 people to get down to 2.5%.

About 95% of the time, the difference between the survey result and the result if you could have surveyed everyone will be less than the sample error.**★★** This rule of

Statistical Snake Oil

Some people claim you can reduce the margin of error in a small survey by performing a very intensive interview with each participant, and using statistical techniques to reduce a large number of answers from each person to a few general metrics.

For example, ask ten people 50 different questions that relate to satisfaction, and boil all the answers down to a single satisfaction metric.

All this technique really does is provide a very accurate measurement of how satisfied those ten people were—but it doesn't allow you to extrapolate their satisfaction to your customer base as a whole. Had Joe been selected for the survey instead of Bob, the results could be very different; and the only way to reduce this effect is to survey more people.

thumb assumes that the survey is much smaller than the total population (if you can survey every customer, there's no sample error). Rather than computing the precise margin of error, most people—even professional statisticians—simply use the rule of thumb. It is, as the saying goes, "close enough for government work." ✱

✱ Unless you happen to be doing government work, in which case the saying is "Close enough for private enterprise."

The good news about sample error is that unlike question bias or sample bias, it is easy (if expensive) to reduce: just survey more people. The bad news is that there is no way to reduce sample error without surveying more people.

The sample error in a survey lets you understand how meaningful a result is. If you run a satisfaction survey in September showing that 75% of your customers are satisfied, and an identical survey in October showing that 80% of your customers are satisfied, should you treat your staff to a fancy dinner or not?

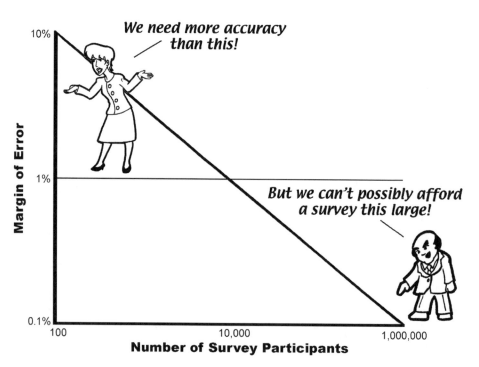

If the margin of error was two points, then the result is very significant, and it's steaks for everyone. On the other hand, if the margin of error was ten points, then the change in satisfaction could easily just be due to statistical fluctuation. If the sample error was five points, then the result is ambiguous (i.e. probably real improvement, but you can't be sure). In this scenario our recommendation is to forget the steaks and order pizza.

Odds of Uncovering Specific Problems

Three Point Mortgage could also be concerned that a bug in its customer service automation is causing problems for some customers. There could be issues with confusing prompts, speech recognition that isn't recognizing speech, language problems, technical bugs, and jargon in recorded messages. These all fall under the general category of usability problems.

For finding usability problems, it is important to examine not just the margin of error in a study, but also the probability of finding a given problem for a given study size.

The severity of a problem is measured by the probability that any given caller will encounter it. For example, a 10% problem could be one that affects 10% of callers at the very beginning of a call, or one that affects 100% of callers on a menu that only 10% of callers hear. A problem that affects more than 10% of callers is severe, and a problem that affects under 1% of callers is relatively minor.

 Even a 1% problem can have a big impact on the operational costs of a call center. Allowing 1% more callers to finish their tasks in a self-service system can save tens of thousands of dollars per month in a high-volume call center.

A problem is "found" in a study if at least five callers report the same problem. In the early stages of developing a new customer service system, a prototype should be tested with an eye to finding major problems. Testing with 50 callers at this stage will find 57% of severe problems which affect 10% of callers; and a 100-person test gets 98% of these problems.

 The threshold of five different callers is arbitrary, but if only one caller experiences a problem it is too easy to dismiss as a fluke.

As development progresses, the size of the tests should increase in order to catch more subtle problems. A 500 person test stands a 97% chance of finding moderately important problems which affect 2% of callers, and a 1,000 person test will catch 97% of the minor problems which affect 1% of callers.

Keep in mind that even in a large study, each test caller represents hundreds or thousands of actual customer calls in a deployed system.

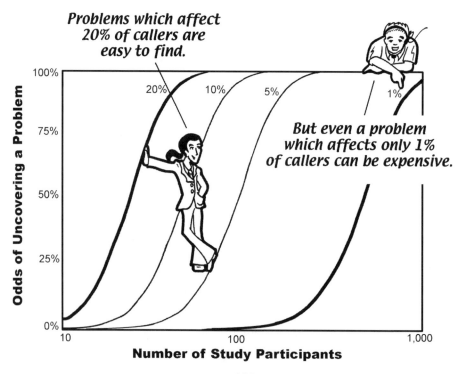

Problems which affect 20% of callers are easy to find.

But even a problem which affects only 1% of callers can be expensive.

112

Usability Testing and Agile Software Development

Extreme Programming (XP) and other "agile" software development methodologies have been a hot topic among programmers for the last several years. Some developers swear they'll never go back to older methods, though others have found insurmountable problems.

Call center applications pose particular challenges when using XP because agile methodologies assume that programmers and users can collaborate to design software. That doesn't work for call centers, since the users are anyone who calls. As a result, formal usability testing is necessary, but traditional usability testing techniques are too cumbersome to work with XP. This appendix has a few ideas for bringing together usability testing and agile development.

Agile Development

Agile methodologies focus on quick turn-around and frequent design/develop/release cycles rather than up-front planning. The idea is to get a minimally useful system up and

113

running as quickly as possible, so that design decisions—including feature requests—are based on practical experience with a working system.

XP depends on speed: speedy design, speedy development, speedy testing, speedy deployment, and quick, informal meetings between developer and client. If any part of a project can't keep up, the other parts pile up like a multicar freeway crash. Therefore every part of XP is optimized for speed:

- Design is done with informal "stories" rather than detailed specifications.

- Development is done in pairs, so that one person programs while the other person reviews the code, designs a test, or looks up information.

- Tests are automated and done primarily on individual software components ("unit testing") rather than the whole system ("functional testing.") Tests are written before the software they test, so programmers can test every time they compile—typically several times in an hour.

- A representative of the client (and, by extension, the users) is part of the development team, serving as a go-to person every time the programmers have a question.

XP can work very well for in-house applications, where the users are employees of the company writing the software. In the best case, the users work down the hall from the programmers, so their feedback can be solicited and incorporated immediately. At worst, there is a representative of the users on hand who is in close contact with many of the users on a regular basis. Agile development is a two-way street: programmers learn about how users are using the program, and at the same time users learn the mindset of the programmers by using the software.

XP and Call Centers

There are two problems with using XP for call center applications. First, the development team typically can't work closely with callers. Second, individual callers often call too infrequently to develop nuanced opinions about the system.

Compounding these problems, usability is much more critical in call centers than other software projects. Callers won't worry about problems with the IVR once they escape to a live agent, but that agent is the most expensive part of the call center. A bad IVR experience is an annoyance to callers, but a major cost to the call center. To put it bluntly, you care about the caller's experience because you depend on callers to make the system work!

Usability testing can bring callers into the design process. Unfortunately, you can't do a traditional lab-based usability test fast enough for XP. Lab tests take days or weeks to schedule, and can cost thousands of dollars each. Nor can you automate usability tests: a human being is inherently part of the process.

The solution is to minimize the time and expense that makes usability testing impractical, and then treat it as a functional test. In the lexicon of XP, functional tests are longer tests that test some feature (or "function") from start to finish. It's common practice to run a complete test suite every night using whatever code is ready.

One approach is to do usability testing with complete regularity. Like automated nightly testing, you schedule one tester per day for the duration of the project, or a few at the same time every week. If the current version of the software isn't ready to test, you find something else to test like a mock-up of a proposed feature. The point is to make usability testing like weekends—something you plan around, not something that can be pushed around.

A more flexible solution is to use rapid assessments. This test method is ideal for combining with functional testing, since it can be done on demand or as part of a daily test suite, and it can be done in as little as one hour.

Usability testing naturally complements unit testing when building customer service applications. Unit testing catches discrepancies between the application and its design. Usability testing catches design flaws. Using techniques like regular usability testing and rapid assessments, we see no reason not to use agile development and usability testing together.

A Glossary of
Call Center Terms

Abandon Rate A statistic often gathered in *call centers*, it measures the percent of callers who hang up while on hold, presumably out of frustration.

Acceptance Test A rigorous shakedown of a new *IVR* or other automated system to make sure it can handle the expected call volume, that callers understand how to use it, and that the vendor can get paid for meeting the terms of its contract.

ACD (Automatic Call Distributor) A phone switch that takes incoming phone calls and distributes them to customer service representatives. Best known for playing the recorded message, "Please hold, your call is very important to us...."

Agent A human being who answers the phone in a *call center*. A call center agent may be the only live representative of your company a customer ever encounters, and can have a profound impact on how customers view your company.

Application Drift The gradual accumulation of small changes to an *IVR* that, over time, can turn a well-designed system into something completely incomprehensible to callers.

ASR (Automated Speech Recognition) see *Speech Recognition*

Audit A very detailed examination of the performance and caller satisfaction levels in a *call center*.

Benchmark A measurement of *call center* performance that is less detailed than an *audit*, and yields a quantitative score intended to compare the performance of a call center to industry standards, another call center, or the same call center at a different time.

Bias An error in a test that systematically gives the same wrong result; for example, because certain callers are excluded from taking a survey, or because a survey question is worded in a way that leads people to choose one answer over the others.

Boneheaded Mistake Something you knew not to do but did anyway, like give the caller fifteen options at the first *IVR menu*, or understaff your *call center* at the busiest time of the year.

Call Center A factory for handling customers' phone calls. The quality of service customers receive is just as much a part of your product as the quality of manufacturing.

Call Logs Detailed records of each call into a *call center*, usually generated by the *IVR, ACD*, and related pieces of equipment. See also *Call Stats*

Call Recording A common quality assurance technique in *call centers* where calls are recorded and used to coach agents or improve an *IVR* system. Call recordings are also common for legal compliance.

Call Stats Statistics generated by a *call center* such as average *time on hold, abandon rate*, and queue depth that give insight into how well a call center is performing. See also *Call Logs*

Caller Satisfaction—also known as Customer Satisfaction. A concept that is simple to describe, except that no two people agree on exactly what it means, and nobody really understands how to measure it. Nevertheless, everyone can agree that it is vitally important to a call center.

Controlled Test A test method for measuring caller opinions of a call center or automated system. The name comes from the fact that the test administrator controls who participates in the study, and what they are asked to do. Controlled tests always involve using a representative group of callers given a particular task to accomplish. This is the most versatile test method, and is often used for *usability testing*, *benchmarking*, and *auditing*.

CRM (Customer Relationship Management) A highly sophisticated combination of databases and powerful software intended to anticipate customers' needs and provide them with the highest possible level of service. Actual results of CRM installations vary.

CSR (Customer Service Representative) see *Agent*

Customer Service That which nearly all companies provide, but that few are good at.

Data Mining Sophisticated statistical techniques used to search for hidden relationships in databases. Data mining can be applied to *call logs* for analysis.

Demo A demonstration of a *call center* or *IVR* for friends, family, employees, or other people with an interest. This yields very little data, but occasionally a demo will be given the more impressive-sounding description *Friends & Family Test*.

End-of-Call Survey A survey administered over the phone at the end of a customer's call. Results from end-of-call surveys are often misleading, since they automatically exclude callers who hang up before the end of the call, and therefore can make the quality of customer service look better than it actually is.

Error (as in *Margin of Error*) Any difference between the results of a test and what actually happens in the real world.

Error occurs for a number of reasons, including imprecise measurements, surveying only a small group of callers, and survey questions that are *biased*.

Expert Opinions Well-informed advice about improving your call center provided by people who are not your customers.

Exploratory Test A preliminary evaluation of a new *VUI* intended to find major problems and design flaws.

Feel-Good Question A survey question that yields no meaningful data, but makes you feel like you're doing a good job.

Follow-Up Survey After annoying a customer with poor service, some *call centers* compound the mistake by calling the customer back—often at home, during dinner—and asking her to take a survey.

Friends & Family Test A test of a call center using friends, family, or employees. See *Demo*.

Gourmet Customer Service The subject of this book: customer service that delights, rather than dismays, your customers. Contrast to *Junk Food Customer Service*.

Grammar In a *speech recognition* system, the words and phrases the software is programmed to recognize at each point in the call.

Humility The hallmark of a seasoned call center testing expert. Newcomers to the field often think they know how real callers feel, but the true experts have learned otherwise.

ICR (Intelligent Call Routing) Technology for routing each caller to the *agent* best able to handle that particular call.

IVR (Interactive Voice Response)—also known as a VRU (Voice Response Unit). An automated system that plays prompts (aka *menus*) to the caller, and responds based on the caller's input. Traditionally input has been through touch-tones, but *speech recognition* is becoming more common.

IVR Containment A *call stat* used to measure how effective an *IVR* is at preventing callers from reaching an *agent*.

Jargon Industry- or company-specific terms that outsiders (i.e. customers) are unlikely to understand. Jargon is one of the most common *usability* problems, since insiders often don't realize they're using specific technical terms.

Junk Food Customer Service The poor quality of service that many consumers have regretfully come to accept as inevitable. While junk food service may answer the customer's immediate need, it rarely does so in a way that leaves customers feeling that they had a worthwhile experience.

Lab Test A *controlled test* that takes place in a laboratory setting.

Large-Scale Test A *controlled test* with hundreds to thousands of participants. Large-scale tests are often used for *auditing*, *benchmarking*, *acceptance testing*, and *mystery shopping*.

Load Test—also known as Stress Test. An automated test where a computer places hundreds or thousands of simulated calls into an *IVR* to make sure it can handle the expected call volume. Often part of an *acceptance test*.

Log Analysis Using statistical tools for turning raw *call logs* into insight about what is actually happening in a *call center* or *IVR* system. Log analysis is more detailed than simply generating *call stats*.

Management Fad-of-the-Week A common technique for trying to improve performance both in the *call center* and throughout the company. Most employees have learned to ignore instructions based on the fad-of-the-week, since they know they will likely receive contradictory orders the following week.

Margin of Error A number that gives the degree of precision in a statistic. By convention, 95% of the time the difference between a statistical measurement and the exact value of what the statistic is measuring should be less than the margin of error.

Mental Model The way a caller thinks your *VUI* works. This often bears little resemblance to the way it actually works.

Menu A list of options in an *IVR* system.

Mystery Shopping A type of *controlled test* where people call anonymously into a call center and evaluate the quality of the *customer service*. The name comes from a similar practice in retail used to check up on both a company's own stores and the competition.

Outsourcer—also known as Service Bureau. Any third party that you pay to handle some or all of your customer calls.

Pilot Test A deployment strategy for rolling out a new automated call center system by sending a percentage of live callers to the new system.

Plumbing Anything that is a routine part of your business, and that you don't need to worry much about. *Customer service* is emphatically **not plumbing**.

Project Lifecycle Typically consists of six phases: Analysis, Design, Coding, Testing, Release, and Operations. Any deployment of call center technology will go through these six phases.

Prototype An early design of a *VUI* intended for testing. Prototypes can be either *working prototypes* or *WOZ* prototypes.

Rapid Assessment A kind of *controlled test* where several dozen participants evaluate a *call center* or *prototype* in a few hours or less.

Reality Check A test that is run for the purpose of making sure a different test is giving reasonable data.

Rules of Thumb—also known as Best Practices or Heuristics. A tried-and-true method for avoiding *boneheaded mistakes* when designing a *VUI* or managing a *call center*. By themselves, rules of thumb are not sufficient to ensure *gourmet customer service*.

Shoot the Messenger What some companies do when faced with bad news.

Speech Recognition Sophisticated software that can understand and respond to spoken words as part of an *IVR* system. The current generation of speech recognition systems are about as intelligent as a golden retriever and just as eager to please.

Task—also known as a Scenario. That which the caller wants to accomplish during his or her call, particularly during a *controlled test*.

Time on Hold A *call stat* often used as a measurement of the quality of *customer service*, since very few customers enjoy waiting on hold. Many things other than hold time influence *caller satisfaction*, so it should not be the exclusive measure of service quality.

Traversal Test A systematic verification that an *IVR* or *speech recognition* system was implemented according to the design.

Tune-Up A program of identifying and implementing simple changes that will improve the performance of a *call center*. Tune-ups can be as short as a few weeks, including testing, analysis, and implementation.

Usability A measure of how easy an automated system is to use. Usability can be hurt by anything that prevents a caller from doing what she needs to do in the call, including poor design, confusing prompts, and technical bugs.

Usability Test Any test, but usually a *Controlled Test*, intended to find *usability* problems with an automated system.

VUI (Voice User Interface) The verbal interface between an *IVR* (particularly one that uses *Speech Recognition*) and the caller. A collective way to refer to all the messages, *grammars*, *menus*, and behaviors the caller will encounter.

Working Prototype—also known as a Functional Prototype or a Rapid Prototype. A prototype of a *VUI* that incorporates actual *speech recognition* and/or touch-tone recognition. Where resources permit, working prototypes are preferred for testing, since they are more realistic than a *WOZ* prototype, and are better suited for large-scale tests.

WOZ (Wizard of Oz) Prototype A mock-up of a *VUI* where a human pretends to be the speech recognition software. The name derives from the fact that in a WOZ test, what appears to be a very impressive piece of technology is nothing more than a man behind a curtain.

For Further Reading

Books

Dillman, Don A.   *Mail and Internet Surveys: The Tailored Design Method,* 2nd Edition, John Wiley & Sons, Inc, 2000; ISBN 0-471-32354-3.

> A thorough book on designing surveys. It contains numerous real-world examples of what can go wrong with a survey and how to avoid errors—including far more kinds of bias than we had time to describe.

Norman, Donald. *The Design of Everyday Things*. Doubleday Books, 1990. Re-issued in 2002 by Basic Books. ISBN 0-465-06710-7.

> The classic book about creating user-friendly designs. This highly readable book outlines a philosophy of design that has influenced everything from coffee pots to the iPod.

Cohen, Michael H; Giangola, James P; and Balogh, Jennifer. *Voice User Interface Design.* Nuance Communications, 2004. ISBN 0-321-18576-5

> A comprehensive text on designing Voice User Interfaces, especially for speech recognition. People designing traditional tone-based IVR will also find this book helpful.

Gonick, Larry; and Smith, Woollcott. *The Cartoon Guide to Statistics.* HarperCollins, 1993. ISBN 0-06-273102-5.

> A nonthreatening, but still comprehensive, introduction to statistics. Despite (or perhaps because of) its lighthearted approach, this is one of the best textbooks and references on general statistics we've seen.

Websites

http://www.vocalabs.com/newsletter/

> Periodic newsletters about testing and measuring the performance of call centers from the authors of this book.

http://www.useit.com/

> Jakob Nielsen's usability website. Geared towards web usability, but with many tips that are also useful in telephony.

http://www.uie.com/articles/

> User Interface Engineering is a counterpoint to UseIt.com. (See http://www.ok-cancel.com/archives/week_2004_02_06.html for a cartoon interpretation of their rivalry.) We like UIE because, like us, it leans toward hard data and statistical relevance, rather than anecdotal case studies and rules of thumb.

Index

Tune-Up 86, 123

U

Usability 123
Usability Tests 11, 33, 123
User Interface, Graphical. *See* GUI
User Interface, Voice. *See* VUI

V

Vendors' Marketing Claims 10, 123
Voice User Interface. *See* VUI
VUI 8, 123

W

Wizard of Oz. *See* WOZ
Working Prototype 25, 89, 123
WOZ 25, 36, 124

About the Authors

Peter and David Leppik are two of the cofounders of Vocal Laboratories Inc. (VocaLabs), a service bureau specializing in measuring the performance of call centers and automated self-service systems using a large panel of consumers.

Peter Leppik is CEO of VocaLabs, and has an extensive background in call center technology financial analysis, and physics. Prior to cofounding VocaLabs he was a financial analyst at the investment bank Dain Rauscher Wessels, researching companies that make call center technology. He holds an MS degree in Physics from the University of Illinois at Urbana-Champaign. Peter is also a licensed pilot, and enjoys spending time hiking near the North Shore of Lake Superior.

David Leppik is VP of Development at VocaLabs, and is an expert in human/computer interaction. Prior to joining VocaLabs, he developed software at NetPerceptions Inc., to personalize websites based on each visitor's anticipated needs. He holds an MS degree in Computer Science from the University of Minnesota. In his free time, he enjoys pencil-and-funny-dice role playing games. The start of this book roughly coincided with the birth of his daughter Sylvia, and he has enthusiastically traded his funny dice for the opportunity to coo, make funny faces, and change diapers.